MW00988623

The Spiral of Memory

POETS ON POETRY · Donald Hall, General Editor

Joy Harjo

The Spiral
of Memory
INTERVIEWS

Edited by Laura Coltelli

Ann Arbor

THE UNIVERSITY OF MICHIGAN PRESS

Copyright © by the University of Michigan 1996
All rights reserved
Published in the United States of America by
The University of Michigan Press
Manufactured in the United States of America
♾ Printed on acid-free paper

1999   1998   1997   1996   4   3   2   1

A CIP catalogue record for this book is available from the British Library.

Library of Congress Cataloging-in-Publication Data

Harjo, Joy.
    The Spiral of memory : interviews / Joy Harjo ; edited by Laura
Coltelli.
        p.   cm. — (Poets on poetry)
    Includes bibliographical references.
    ISBN 0-472-09581-1 (hardcover : alk. paper). — ISBN 0-472-06581-5
(pbk. : alk. paper)
    1. Harjo, Joy—Interviews.   2. Women poets, American—20th
century—Interviews.   3. Authors, Indian—20th century—Interviews.
4. Navajo Indians in literature.   5. Navajo women—Interviews.
6. Arizona—In literature.   7. Poetry—Authorship.   8. Poetics.
I. Coltelli, Laura, 1941–   .   II. Title.   III. Series.
PS3558.A62423Z466 1996
811'.54—dc20   95-40043
                                                                CIP

Contents

Introduction

The Transforming Power of Joy Harjo's Poetry

by Laura Coltelli

Joy Harjo is one of the more powerful voices among the second generation of the so-called Native American Renaissance, the movement that arose in the late 1960s with N. Scott Momaday, James Welch, and Leslie Marmon Silko. Through these works, extraordinarily innovative in content but also in form, these Indian writers for the first time bore witness directly to their native world, interpreting it from within and freeing it from the portrayals by white writers that had been at best ambivalent, if not thoroughly distorted. The arduous, agonizing reconstruction of the tribal past, the dramatic confrontation with white civilization, the existential and artistic itinerary through present-day America, the shady liminal area inhabited by mixed-bloods—such are the major themes of a literary corpus that has now grown to considerable proportions, one that within a span of thirty years has been acclaimed by critics and readers alike for its vitality and its prodigious variety of voices and styles.

Joy Harjo has to date completed six poetry collections, the most recent of which is the newly published *The Woman Who Fell from the Sky*. This latest collection, which came out while the present group of interviews was already in progress, is destined to kindle a fresh round of in-depth conversations with the author, for it infuses new depth into her poetry, further extending and enhancing the kaleidoscopic multicultural background and the multiple layering of her poetic voice. Since the appearance in 1975 of her first collection, *The Last Song,* Joy Harjo has unwaveringly pursued a personal and artistic calling with a profundity of vision that has shaped her work into a deeply felt, aching testimony endowed with integrity and suffused with the spirit of renewal.

Born in Tulsa, Oklahoma, in 1951, to a young mother of mixed Cherokee and French blood scarcely out of childhood and a Creek father descended from an outstanding family of speakers and leaders, Harjo herself became the mother of two children at a very early age, whom she brought up amid suffering and hardship. Her first poetic compositions were written when she was twenty-two, after she had moved to the Southwest and had attended a fine arts course at the Institute of American Indian Arts of Santa Fe. Later she received her B.A. from the University of New Mexico in 1976, and her M.F.A. from the University of Iowa's Writers' Workshop in 1978. She has taught Native American literature and creative writing at the Institute of American Indian Arts, Arizona State University, the University of Colorado at Boulder, the University of Arizona at Tucson, and is currently tenured at the University of New Mexico at Albuquerque. Her creative abilities encompass not only poetry but scriptwriting, filmmaking, and playing a "tribal-jazz-reggae."

Active in a number of organizations devoted to the spread of native cultures, Joy Harjo has also long displayed a commitment to editorial work. Her achievements as an editor have now culminated in a monumental and valuable anthology, *Reinventing the Enemy's Language*—the publication of which is awaited with eagerness—charting the contribution of women writers belonging to tribal communities throughout the world.

An eclectic commitment of this stature, over a multiplicity of fields of action, is reflected in Harjo's poetry, which is likewise multilayered and increasingly suffused with profound interconnections among the various elements of which her poems are composed.

Her ethnic background deeply affects her relationship with the land as it is described or felt in her poems, since "the American Indian has a unique investment in the American landscape," to use one of Scott Momaday's maxims in this regard, an investment that means perhaps thirty thousand years of habitations and experience of the American continent.[1] This ethical idea of the land is always at work in Harjo's poetry. It is an ancient appropriation and perception of the earth that stems from her native culture, in reverence and wonder, confidence and comprehension.

Harjo's first poetical works were linked above all to Oklahoma, of which she herself speaks in an essay significantly entitled "Oklahoma: The Prairie of Words":

> All of the people, all of the voices who are from Oklahoma, remain part of that spirit. Even if they move away they always return. They return, even if they have been sent miles away to school or leave to find jobs, and then come back with families and settle down. Some return only during the moist, humid summers to the dancing, warm drum nights near towns named Anadarko, Henryetta, Miami, or to the numerous other grounds. And some return only in their hearts and voices, singing, again and again—to Oklahoma red earth, a curved wind plain—to creeks and rivers that cross over and through the land. No one has ever left.[2]

But the Southwest itself is also a place of absolute centrality, as is well illustrated by *Secrets from the Center of the World,* in which Harjo weaves the web of a passionate dialogue with Stephen Strom's outstanding photographs. The essence of Strom's shots lies in eschewing any facile reliance on the spectacular depth of perspective of the wide open spaces characteristic of the American landscape, impressive though such a setting may be. Refraining from the sometimes hackneyed scenic depth shots, the vast expanse is instead condensed into a miniature dimension, so that our eye, instead of losing itself in a cliché of immensity, is obliged to look at it with focus on the particular. And it is on these particulars that Harjo's poetry centers, intensely seeking to affirm that the knowledge of physical roots is the knowledge of spiritual belonging. "The land took me in," Harjo continues, in response to inquiries in this regard, "especially when I tried to find my way out of chaos, fed me so much and fed me well. *Secrets* became for me a way of giving back." Here too, then, as well as in a continuous intimate dialogue, the existence of a reciprocal relationship characteristic of Indian cultures is proclaimed. And in the immensity of nature, which in Western culture represents the place par excellence where the sense of self is lost, Harjo does not forget herself, but on the contrary rediscovers her identity.

Just as Strom's photographs are not illustrations, but pictures, so also Harjo's works are not vaguely poeticized captions but the evocation of the spirit of the place. The picture and the word are not in competition with each other, but rather proceed side by side for the very good reason that the absolute protagonist is *this* earth, *this* landscape, *this* atmosphere. The words and pictures are there to underline them and perhaps to free them from the déjà vu of dramatic spectacles that trivialize the majesty of a landscape so famous, yet ultimately so unknown. While Strom maintains a respectful distance with his lens, Harjo writes: "This land is a poem of ochre and burnt sand I could never write, unless paper were the sacrament of sky, and ink the broken line of wild horses staggering the horizon several miles away" (p. 30). And these lines, and others, contain a sharply focused declaration of poetics: her poetry is not to be taken as a visual or descriptive poetry, but rather as evocative, like this earth inhabited by creatures that are not manifested but are within it, are the earth itself. Like the horses that are pink sand (p. 42), the crows that are tamerisks (p. 20), and like Harjo who saw herself recreated in that land (p. 52) and who in the winter of that land sees her own death (p. 34). It is an autobiographical land in the sense that within it there lives and breathes the entire history and mythic framework of a people, a people that at a certain point becomes the whole of humanity and whose goings-on are crystallized in stratifications of rock (p. 46). Thus appearances dissolve and the presences emerge; the spaces become truly inhabited even if we have no precise silhouettes before our eyes: for these shapes are not entities that trivially materialize before us, but entities that live diffused in the external world just as they are also internal to the individual.[3]

In her poetry, the sense of the perennial movement from

one place to the other as it is reflected from one poem to the next is not the senseless wandering of the uprooted, but instead traces an itinerary that bears a deep identification with the land, a geography of the remembered earth that in Harjo's poetry takes on three physical directions, specular and complementary to one another. This *itinerarium mentis* sets out from Oklahoma, the red earth where she was born, the embodiment of family and tribe, and proceeds in the direction of the Southwest and the desert landscape, not barren and parched but full of life, and which in many instances conveys the sense of a mythic womanhood to defeat harsh realities; the third direction centers on Alabama, where the Creek tribe lived before the Indian Removal Act, a land that is the original place, lost forever and forever created in the original memory.

But the landscape described by Harjo also has a specific reference point in the contemporary American city, which harshly gives shape to that sense of indifference, hostility, social, and psychological alienation:

> Within her varied urban landscape, Harjo's poetry most clearly illustrates the multivoiced nature of any marginalized poetry, and of Native American women's poetry in particular. On one hand, after a first reading, Harjo may seem to be writing out of the city-as-subject tradition of American poets like Walt Whitman, Carl Sandburg, Hart Crane, and William Carlos Williams. On the other hand, her city landscapes do not reflect promise and optimistic excitement, as do many urban settings of earlier white male American poets. Rather, Harjo's cities resonate with Native American memories of an endless and ongoing history of Eurocentric and genocidal social and political policies: war, forced removal, imposed education, racism, and assimilationism.[4]

This sense of closure, which does not refer only to urban landscapes, finds expression in the innumerable images of borders, constantly crossed and constantly present. This implies not only the struggle for poetic and personal self-realization but also an attempt to affirm an essential unity of things that is specifically Indian. Thus the structure of *She Had Some Horses* indicates "a cyclical pattern of union, loss, separation and longing; the journey for recovered experience; and the reunion, only temporary, after which there begins again the cyclic quest of a voice looking for home."[5]

In *Mad Love and War* this quest is re-presented and further perspectives are opened up. To an Indian legacy of struggles Harjo adds the lucid awareness of a contemporary world smoldering with conflicts that threaten to flare up into a blaze. She thus directs her attention not to one particular place, but to a "global village." Through such an approach, individual or ethnic conflict can be overcome, and an avenue opened up to dissolution of the first among the many barriers that are encountered in a multicultural situation. It is thus that the "war" present in the title dilates and becomes "the wars" of the initial part of the collection: these are conflicts occurring on every side, small or large scale, declared hostilities or rumbling standoffs, public and private conflicts, and above all racial conflicts investing whole nations or single individuals in a universe in which "there are no words for how the real world / collapses" ("Deer Dancer"). But there is also the silent war of marginalization and desolation. The wars Harjo presents are stratified over time, veining "the backbone of these / tortuous Americas" ("The Real Revolution Is Love"), peopled by the dead who are not dead, by tribal warriors and victims of modern alienation, mythic figures of ravaging forces, hooded ghosts, precarious and desperate family predicaments.

The second part, "Mad Love," indicates the continuation of the journey, from fragmentation to completeness: an itinerary that brings no solace, and does not lead to oblivion—"Nothing can be forgotten, only left behind" ("Autobiography"). It draws its healing impulse from the intense existence of things "larger than the memory / of a dispossessed people," of lands and people lost and found again with an unbroken communicative endeavor "in the epic search for grace" ("Grace"). The larger memory, as Harjo herself asserts, "is the memory of ourselves as we were before destruction and as we survive."[6]

And it is precisely at this point that the rich thematic density of Harjo's poetry develops along channels already foreshadowed but not fully explored in the previous collections. Development unfolds in the direction of overcoming other barriers, so that these poems become a poetry of metamorphosis and urge for transformation, with all vital forces striving toward renewal. The itinerary now sets out from survival and leads into growth, from bearing witness to history into active participation, from identification of distance to the striving to obliterate the gap.

The path tracked by Harjo is that of a new resistance, different from static resistance to history or to that "winter in the blood"—to cite the title of the novel by the Blackfeet writer James Welch, to whom "Grace" is dedicated—which paralyzes the convergence of diverse cultural backgrounds, freezes memory, and separates the past from the present. For such a static vision, as has frequently been observed, would ultimately leave the Indian trapped in his own museum: "I learned a long time ago, after much difficulty and near suicide, that I would not allow the duality of blood to destroy me. . . . This racial/identity split is another device by the colonizer to destroy us."[7]

This new regenerating perspective endows one of the central metaphors of Harjo's poetry with a new dimension. As we have seen, motion stands at the heart of her poetry: it is a journey both physical and spiritual that prepares for a meeting with the other, and for a different meeting with one's own self, "another viewpoint on the density of life."[8] This appears even more important if surveyed, as does the writer herself, "in the light of the removal of the Muscogee people from Alabama to Oklahoma. It was a forced walk away from our original homeland. Perhaps that is also why I am always traveling."[9]

But even if the ancient stories that bestow identity on a people occurred in a different landscape, Harjo goes on, "I suppose the heart will always lead you where you are supposed to go, whether it be in Oklahoma, Alabama or Arizona. The original impulse of those stories pumps your blood."[10] Harjo's manifold journeys have their source within a history that is as individual as it is collective, "blowing like wind across cultures and landscapes she writes about,"[11] as for instance in the exemplary "A Winning Hand," where the wind is an inner force, "a vehicle for movement, exploration, erosion."[12]

Thus if in *What Moon Drove Me to This* the key word is "edge," and this is repeated again in *She Had Some Horses*, albeit within a different perspective, in *In Mad Love and War* the key word is "transformation," which is not circumscribed in one single word but is transformation into that of which the poems speak, transformation of language with other words and beyond words, transformation of anger while preserving it—not forgetting it—as Harjo says, citing Ghandi, "so our anger, controlled, can be transmitted into power which can move the world."[13]

Despite carrying within herself the memory of precarious existential situations and diverse cultural heritages, Joy Harjo believes that it is indispensable to set out on a quest—often desperate and furious but never futile or conciliating—in order to seek a new vision of herself and the world that will allow development of bonds and connections, so that a principle of reciprocity can be affirmed, traversing history and myths to renew them in continuity.

And if there is an Indian legacy of struggles, there is also an Indian heritage that proclaims the interrelatedness of all things, the cyclical flow of all events, the union of the animate and inanimate world, the final convergence of processes governing personal and collective concerns. Aware of these multiple patterns, so intimately connected, Joy Harjo thus molds her poetic testimony.

At the core of this quest there lies the never-ending interaction between past and present, or the watchful attention of mythic figures, who reappear in her interviews—projections of different worlds that absorb into their being the experience of mystery yet can be controlled by a culture because they have been blended into the ancient stories. They have come to form an integral part of the heritage through which the wisdom and experience of a people are handed down from one generation to another; they embody the sense of belonging to a community, to a land, to a past that flows without discontinuity into the present.

Joy Harjo allows us, in the most appropriate manner, to share in this heritage, as indicated by Adrienne Rich:

She's generous in her poetry, opening her sacred spaces and music to all, yet never naive or forgetful about hostility and hatred, as in "Transformations." . . . This is not forgiveness, turning the cheek. It's a claiming of power, the power of the poetic act, the courage and grace and knowledge it takes to reach, through "the right words, the right meaning" into that place in the other where "the most precious animals leave." It's about "tough belief," no sentimental gesturing. You hear it in the rhythms of Harjo's music, catching it in the bladed outlines of her images.[14]

This same energy provides nourishment for memory, which strives to retrace the past not as an inducement to curl inwards on oneself, as if it were a point in time without escape route, but rather as a dynamic process to reaffirm ancient heritages and proceed forward on a path of constant renewal:

> The way I see remembering, just the nature of the word, had to do with going back. But I see it another way, too. I see it as occurring, not just going back, but occurring right now, and also future occurrence. . . .[15]

What affords the most successful figurative description of the proceeding of memory is the spinning movement of the vortex, which spirals down the tip while simultaneously expanding toward the future like the spiral in "Heartshed": "in the beginning / It doesn't mean going backward. / Our bones are built of spirals."

In a "ceremonial spiral of prayer" ("Original Memory") and with a "spiraling dance" ("Autobiography"), the mythic world is re-evoked and ritualized. The linearity of the chronological sequence of time dissolves in the "mythic spiral of time" ("Hieroglyphic"), which breaks down the divisions and fragmentations of memory ("Four years isn't long on this spiral of tangential stories" ["Death Is a Woman"]), and recaptures images and existences "Just the other side of this room of whirling atoms" ("Death Is a Woman"), or follows invisible connections in a frenzied rush on "a spiral arc through an Asiatic burst of time" ("Nine Below"). And all this is in turn encompassed within other greater connections, such as "the structure of the spiraled world" ("Nine Lives"), "the spiral of the sky above it" ("We Must Call a Meeting"), or a vortex that contains us together with "a laughing god / swimming the heavens" ("Fury of Rain").

The responsibility with which memory is invested thus determines an impulse toward transformation, as indeed emerges from many of Harjo's comments to the various interviewers. And since this memory is at once collective and individual, each sphere becomes the object of this metamorphosis, renewing the bond between the world of myths and personal happenings, as in the recollection of the birth of her daughter in "Rainy Dawn."

If the previous collection *She Had Some Horses,* although setting out along the path toward acquisition of a new identity, still portrayed memory as "a delta in the skin," in *In Mad Love and War* memory becomes "a revolutionary fire." And more than ever, more even than in *Horses,* memory affects the sphere of language, a subject that occupies an important position in the interviews presented here. Memory strips down yet at the same time enhances—indeed dilates—the potentialities of language itself, to the point of producing visions of unrelenting, surreal density in "Santa Fe," or of explosive chromatic compactness as in "City of Fire," or the oneiric evocativeness of "Nine Below."

Such complex utilization of language gives rise to a number of questions in the interviews concerning individual words and the semantic stratifications linked to them, but also extending to inquiry into the genesis of some of the poems and the imagery that pervades them.

Harjo also attends to the relation between the oral tradition and written literature, as well as that between minority literatures and the mainstream Anglo-American literary tradition. Other subjects include the contribution minority literature has made to the mainstream tradition, and the enrichment deriving from professors and individual writers. In a writer whose work is "woman-identified," we feel that considerable clarification is provided by Harjo's statement concerning feminism, namely that it "doesn't carry over to the tribal world, but a concept mirroring a similar meaning would . . . —empowerment, some kind of empowerment. . . . I feel connected to others, but many women's groups have a majority of white women and I honestly can feel uncomfortable, or even voiceless sometimes."[16]

Specific analysis of Harjo's poetic technique frequently prompts a revisitation of the cultural background from whence she comes. The frequent use of repetition, for instance, is thus not to be taken as a mere device, but rather as "a definite acknowledgement of ceremony . . ."; indeed it "always elicits that sense of ceremony": "in any kind of ceremonial action, ceremonial pronouncements, the repetition always backs up, enforces the power of what you've said."[17]

Within the collection as a whole, some of the questions inevitably overlap, on account of the centrality of certain specific themes within Harjo's poetry. It is nevertheless incontestable that each answer contributes to enriching the picture with further valuable details, gradually building up a mosaic that brings into ever sharper focus Harjo as a poet and Harjo as an artist. This is the case, for instance, whenever she mentions some specific elements of an autobiographical nature or when she dwells on the image of horses or on the fundamental role of memory. Furthermore, the degree of emphasis with which she responds to some of the questions repeatedly put to her allows one to sense something like an evolution, discernible as regards the thematic aspects but also of a more general nature. There are glimpses here and there of new avenues being opened up, in a continuous exploration of the self and the surrounding environment. This is particularly noticeable in that "ongoing process of discovery" in search of "new psychic splits of space."[18]

Emblematic in this connection is Harjo's statement in the interviews closest to us in time concerning the importance of music, and jazz in particular, for her work: for between the art of poetry and the art of music, she significantly states, "there is not . . . a separation in tribal cultures."[19]

"The space has grown larger," she says à propos of her recent production, and the testimony she offers in her interviews confirms this growth. This constant striving toward renewal, often fraught with difficulties but steadfastly pursued, has accompanied her throughout her journey—of which she speaks in "Autobiography"—from "that ragged self . . . chased through precarious years," to the culminating point of imagining "a promise made when no promise was possible," as she says in "Promise of Blue Horses," appearing in her latest collection, *The Woman Who Fell from the Sky.*

NOTES

1. N. Scott Momaday, "A First American Views His Land," *National Geographic Magazine* 105, no. 1 (1976): 14. See also "An American Land Ethic," *Sierra Club Bulletin* 55, no. 2 (1970): 8–11.

2. Joy Harjo, "Oklahoma: The Prairie of Words," in Geary Hobson ed., *The Remembered Earth: An Anthology of Contemporary Native American Literature* (Albuquerque: Red Earth Press, 1979), 45.

3. This part concerning *Secrets from the Center of the World* and the following part on *In Mad Love and War* are partially dealt with in my introductions to the Italian edition of the above-mentioned works published by the Quattroventi Press of Urbino, 1992 and 1995.

4. Nancy Lang, "Twin Gods Bending Over: Joy Harjo and Poetic Memory," *Melus* 18, no. 3 (Fall 1993): 41–42.

5. Andrew Wiget, "Nightriding with Noni Daylight: The Many Horse Songs of Joy Harjo," in Laura Coltelli, ed., *Native American Literatures* (Pisa: Seu, 1989), 186.

6. "The Spectrum of Other Languages," this volume, p. 106.

7. Ibid., p. 106.

8. "Landscape and the Place Inside," this volume, p. 75.

9. Ibid., p. 75.

10. Ibid., p. 76.

11. Sidner Larson, "*In Mad Love and War,*" *American Indian Quarterly* 15, no. 2 (Spring 1991): 273.

12. Ibid., p. 273.

13. "The Story of All Our Survival," this volume, p. 26.

14. Adrienne Rich, "The World of Women," *Ms.* 70 (Sept.–Oct. 1991): 73.

15. "The Story of All Our Survival," this volume, p. 24.
16. "The Circular Dream," this volume, pp. 65, 66.
17. "Landscape and the Place Inside," this volume, p. 84.
18. "Horses, Poetry, and Music," this volume, p. 89.
19. Ibid., p. 90.

The Creative Process

The Woman Hanging from the Thirteenth Floor Window

She is the woman hanging from the 13th floor
window. Her hands are pressed white against the
concrete moulding of the tenement building. She
hangs from the 13th floor window in east Chicago,
with a swirl of birds over her head. They could
be a halo, or a storm of glass waiting to crush her.

She thinks she will be set free.

The woman hanging from the 13th floor window
on the east side of Chicago is not alone.
She is a woman of children, of the baby, Carlos,
and of Margaret, and of Jimmy who is the oldest.
She is her mother's daughter and her father's son.
She is several pieces between the two husbands
she has had. She is all the women of the apartment
building who stand watching her, watching themselves.

When she was young she ate wild rice on scraped down
plates in warm wood rooms. It was in the farther
north and she was the baby then. They rocked her.

She sees Lake Michigan lapping at the shores of
herself. It is a dizzy hole of water and the rich
live in tall glass houses at the edge of it. In some
places Lake Michigan speaks softly, here, it just sputters
and butts itself against the asphalt. She sees
other buildings just like hers. She sees other
women hanging from many-floored windows

From *Wicazo Sa Review* 1, no. 1 (Spring 1985):38–40.

counting their lives in the palms of their hands
and in the palms of their children's hands.

She is the woman hanging from the 13th floor window
on the Indian side of town. Her belly is soft from
her children's births, her worn levis swing down below
her waist, and then her feet, and then her heart.
She is dangling.

The woman hanging from the 13th floor hears voices.
They come to her in the night when the lights have gone
dim. Sometimes they are little cats mewing and scratching
at the door, sometimes they are her grandmother's voice,
and sometimes they are gigantic men of light whispering
to her to get up, to get up, to get up. That's when she wants
to have another child to hold onto in the night, to be able
to fall back into dreams.

And the woman hanging from the 13th floor window
hears other voices. Some of them scream out from below
for her to jump, they would push her over. Others cry softly
from the sidewalks, pull their children up like flowers and gather
them into their arms. They would help her, like themselves.

But she is the woman hanging from the 13th floor window,
and she knows she is hanging by her own fingers, her
own skin, her own thread of indecision.

She thinks of Carlos, of Margaret, of Jimmy.
She thinks of her father, and of her mother.
She thinks of all the women she has been, of all
the men. She thinks of the color of her skin, and
of Chicago streets, and of waterfalls and pines.
She thinks of moonlight nights, and of cool spring storms.
Her mind chatters like neon and northside bars.
She thinks of the 4 a.m. lonelinesses that have folded
her up like death, discordant, without logical and
beautiful conclusion. Her teeth break off at the edges.
She would speak.

The woman hangs from the 13th floor window crying for
the lost beauty of her own life. She sees the
sun falling west over the grey plane of Chicago.
She thinks she remembers listening to her own life

break loose, as she falls from the 13th floor
window on the east side of Chicago, or as she
climbs back up to claim herself again.

How did this poem begin?

This poem began two years before I began writing it, during
a trip to Chicago to visit friends, see the King Tut exhibit
and look for other Indians. I found the Chicago Indian Cen-
ter at nearly dusk. It could have been any other urban In-
dian center, the same part of the city, a color like lost dreams,
air tasting like a borrowed hope, and always the ragged pool
tables where kids acting twice their age shoot pool downhill
all day.

One particular image stayed with me for two years, and it
probably wasn't exactly what I saw, but changed, transformed
with living. And it wasn't the most significant image I remem-
ber, or it didn't appear to be, but something about that one
small room, hardly anyone in it, a western window with no
curtains, maybe a few toothless venetian blinds, and a rocking
chair, especially that bony rocking chair with stuffing coming
out of the padding, and the sun falling behind a horizon of
skyscrapers, triggered the poem, the story in it.

What still strikes me about the remembering is not know-
ing whether "for real" anyone had been rocking in that rock-
ing chair, but everytime I remember it I remember a young
woman nursing a baby, or an old man with a greasy paper sack
on his knee, softly breathing: or two kids rocking it hard and
being warned to slow down; or that old woman at forty who
watched the sunset as receding light across the floor; or the
other one laughing at her sister's terrible jokes; or anyone I
may have seen or not seen in that rocking chair.

The woman hanging from the thirteenth floor window
could have been in that chair, just hours before, letting that
steady rhythm calm her, a heartbeat against wood, trying to
dream her own regeneration, so that any kind of hopelessness
wouldn't be overwhelming.

Out of this the poem took root, two years before the actual
writing began.

I wrote the poem one afternoon as I sat at my desk in my office at the Institute of American Indian Arts in Santa Fe, after I pulled out a sheath of papers one of which had a note on it about the Chicago Indian Center, something quickly scribbled about the rocking chair, that room.

It was probably one of the quicker poems I have written, in terms of getting its basic structure down, the basic line of it. And unusual in the sense that I kept feeling her there, standing behind me, urging me on.

What changes did you make?

I don't recall all the changes I made after the first draft of the poem, but there were many. I probably wound up with at least twenty pages of revision and then some. These days when I write it's even more revision. To me that is much of the art of writing, the craft of it, taking care that the language fits, that what is meant is clear in terms of what is evoked in the reader, the listener, and what is spoken is said so beautifully even when speaking into moments/events that I have to painfully see.

As a poet I feel that it is my responsibility to be clear and alive in my work, to not add to the confusion.

What techniques did you use?

One technique I often use, and use in "The Woman Hanging from the Thirteenth Floor Window" is that of repetition. For me it is a way of speaking that can, if used effectively, make the poem lift off the page and enter into the listener much like a song or a chant. Repetition has always been used, ceremonially, in telling stories, in effective speaking, so that what is said becomes a litany, and gives you a way to enter into what is being said, and a way to emerge whole, but changed.

Also important as to why a certain technique would be appealing to a particular poet and/or poem has much to do with background, culture, family histories. What I call my influences in terms of writing are a combination of many musics, including: country western songs, like the ones my mother played on the radio, jukeboxes and often sang around the house; preaching, such as that done by Creek preachers, like that one of my Creek grandfather Henry Marsey Harjo; Creek Stomp Dance songs; jazz, which I know my tribe had something to do with its beginnings, coming like we do from Alabama and places south, just listen to our music; early Motown we played at Indian school, danced to it and knew all the words; and always the heartbreaking blues.

Who is your audience?

Who I saw when I closed my eyes and wrote this poem were women, mostly Indian women, those who survived and those who weren't strong enough (whose words we'll always have to carry), the ones who speak through me, and even those who hate me for speaking. I saw women who were holding many children, others embracing lovers, some dancing the stomp dance, and others swinging hard out on some spinning dance floor. Heard much weeping, and even more laughter.

I think I always write with especially these women in mind because I want us all to know as women, as Indian people, as human beings that there is always hope, that we are whole, alive, and precious.

Can this poem be paraphrased?

Yes. It is basically easy to paraphrase, whereas other poems I have written would be nearly impossible to paraphrase. It goes like this: an Indian woman from Wisconsin who has come into Chicago to make a living, because she can't at home, is hanging by her hands from her apartment building. She is desperate, feels alone, and at the moment the poem begins has difficulty seeing her life fit clearly, with any kind of beautiful meaning.

She watches her life pass in front of her. Thinks especially of her children, and of her home, and knows that where she is from Lake Michigan speaks another tone of voice because she has sat on the lake shore and listened long and hard to the stories. Here in Chicago, Lake Michigan speaks more desperately as it slams itself against the concrete along the edge of the waterfront. She, too, feels the city as abrupt, hard.

She sees people gather below her and knows herself as many of the women who are watching. Even though there are those who are screaming for her to jump I like to feel she sees other possibilities in those who, "pull their children up like flowers and gather them into their arms," in those who remember life, and can tell their own survival.

The end of the poem I left deliberately ambiguous. The listener doesn't know whether she jumped, or whether she pulled herself back up. I've always like stories that were able to accomplish that kind of ending well. There aren't too many of them. "The Lady or the Tiger" is one. That kind of ending can work as long as there is still a resolution in the ambiguity.

A personal comment: Many people have come up to me after a poetry reading and asked me about this woman who was hanging from the thirteenth floor window, because they were sure they knew her, or one of her cousins, her sister, or they had read about the story in the newspaper where they lived, be it New York or Lincoln, Nebraska, or Albuquerque. It was familiar to them, haunted them after hearing the poem because it evoked some possible memory.

I know there is a woman; perhaps many women are this woman. And you know her, or thought you did, or will. Because it's a story that has happened; perhaps it's happening now.

The Story of All Our Survival

Interview with Joseph Bruchac

Anchorage

for Audre Lorde

This city is made of stone, of blood, and fish,
There are Chugatch Mountains to the east
and whale and seal to the west.
It hasn't always been this way, because glaciers
who are ice ghosts create oceans, carve earth
and shape this city here, by the sound.
They swim backwards in time.

Once a storm of boiling earth cracked open
the streets, threw open the town.
It's quiet now, but underneath the concrete
is the cooking earth,
                    and above that, air
which is another ocean, where spirits we can't see
are dancing   joking   getting full
on roasted caribou, and the praying
goes on, extends out.

Nora and I go walking down 4th Avenue
and know it is all happening.
On a park bench we see someone's Athabascan
grandmother, folded up, smelling like 200 years
of blood and piss, her eyes closed against some
unimagined darkness, where she is buried in an ache
in which nothing makes
                    sense.

From Joseph Bruchac, *Survival This Way: Interviews with American Indian Poets,* Tucson: University of Arizona Press, 1987.

We keep on breathing, walking, but softer now,
the clouds whirling in the air above us.
What can we say that would make us understand
better than we do already?
Except to speak of her home and claim her
as our own history, and know that our dreams
don't end here, two blocks away from the ocean
where our hearts still batter away at the muddy shore.

And I think of the 6th Avenue jail, of mostly Native
and Black men, where Henry told about being shot at
eight times outside a liquor store in L.A., but when
the car sped away he was surprised he was alive,
no bullet holes, man, and eight cartridges strewn
on the sidewalk
                    all around him.

Everyone laughed at the impossibility of it,
but also the truth. Because who would believe
the fantastic and terrible story of all of our survival
those who were never meant
                    to survive?

I'm glad you started with that poem, Joy. Those last few lines, the "story of all of our survival, / those who were never meant to survive," are pretty much the theme I see as central in contemporary American Indian poetry: the idea of survival. What are you saying in this poem about survival?

I see it almost like a joke, the story about Henry in the poem I just read. You know, he was real dry when he was talking about standing out there and all those bullet holes and he's lying on the ground and he thought for sure he'd been killed but he was alive and telling the story and everybody laughed because they thought he was bullshitting. And it's like a big joke that any of us are here because they tried so hard to make sure we weren't, you know, either kill our spirits, move us from one place to another, try to take our minds and our hearts.

That poem has many storied tied into it, stories of people that you know, stories of women, stories of things that you remember. Storytelling seems to run through and even structure much of the work by American Indian poets. Is that true for you?

I rely mostly on contemporary stories. Even though the older ones are like shadows or are there dancing right behind them, I know that the contemporary stories, what goes on now, will be those incorporated into those older stories or become a part of that. It's all still happening. A lot of contemporary American native writers consciously go back into the very old traditions, and I think I do a lot unconsciously. I don't think I'm a good storyteller in that sense, but it's something that I'm learning. I love to hear them and use them in my own ways.

If there's an image of the American Indian writer that many people, who are not very knowledgeable about what an American Indian writer is, have, it is of what I call jokingly the Beads and Feathers School, nineteenth-century "noble savages." The poetry in this new book of yours is not Beads and Feathers, yet to me it's very recognizably from an American Indian consciousness. What is that consciousness?

I suppose it has to do with a way of believing or sensing things. The world is not disconnected or separate but whole. All persons are still their own entity but not separate from everything else—something that I don't think is necessarily just Native American, on this particular continent, or only on this planet. All people are originally tribal, but Europeans seem to feel separated from that, or they've forgotten it. If European people look into their own history, their own people were tribal societies to begin with and they got away from it. That's called "civilization."

Leslie Silko and Geary Hobson have both attacked the phenomenon of the "White Shaman," the Anglo poet who writes versions of American Indian poems. What are your thoughts on that?

I agree with them. It's a matter of respect to say, "I'm borrowing this from this place," or "I'm stealing this from here," or "I'm making my own poem out of this," but the white shamans don't do that. They take something and say it's theirs or they take the consciousness and say it's theirs, or try to steal the spirit. On one hand, anybody can do what they want but they pay the consequences. You do have to have that certain respect, and you do have to regard where things come from and to whom they belong.

Origins are very important in your work. Where things came from, where you came from. The title of your first book is The Last Song, *and you ended it with "oklahoma will be the last song / I'll ever sing." Is it not true that you have in your work a very strong sense of yourself as a person from a place which informs you as a writer?*

I suppose. But the older I get the more I realize it's caused a great deal of polarity within myself. I recognized my roots, but at the same time there's a lot of pain involved with going back. I've thought about it many times, like why I travel, why I'm always the wanderer in my family. One of the most beloved members of my family died just recently, my aunt Lois Harjo. She always lived in Oklahoma, and I've jokingly said the reason I'm always traveling is so that Andrew Jackson's troops don't find me. You know, they moved my particular family from Alabama to Oklahoma, and so I always figure I stay one step ahead so they can't find me.

Some American Indian writers—you and Barney Bush, for example—are the epitome, for me, of the poets who are always on the move, going from one place to another. Yet I still find a very strong sense in your work and in Barney's that you are centered in place. You are not nomads. There's a difference between your moving around and the way people in Anglo society are continually moving, always leaving something behind.

Oh, it's because in their sense they're always moving to get away from their mothers. They don't want to be from here or there. It's a rootlessness. But there will always be place and family and roots.

Those are things which you come back to in your work: those connections to family, to memory. A poem of yours is called "Remember." I think that's very important. The idea of remembering is central, isn't it, in the work of many, many American Indian writers?

The way I see remembering, just the nature of the word, has to do with going back. But I see it in another way, too. I see it as occurring, not just going back, but occurring right now, and also future occurrence so that you can remember things in a way that makes what occurs now beautiful. I don't see it as going back and dredging up all kinds of crap or all kinds of past romance. People are people, whatever era, whoever they are, they're people.

In other words, memory is alive for you. You're not just engaged in a reverie—like the old man sitting by the fire and going back over those things in the past. Memory is a living and strong force which affects the future.

Sure. People often forget that everything they say, everything they do, think, feel, dream, has effect, which to me is being Indian, knowing that. That's part of what I call "being Indian" or "tribal consciousness."

You also talk in your poems about the importance of saying things, speaking. What is speaking for you? What I'm asking, really, is for you to define words I see being used by American Indian writers very differently than most people use them. Song is one of those words. Memory is one of those words. Speaking is one of those words.

It comes out of the sense of not being able to speak. I still have a sense of not being able to say things well. I think much of the problem is with the English language; it's a very materialistic and a very subject-oriented language. I don't know Creek, but I know a few words and I am familiar with other tribal languages more so than I am my own. What I've noticed is that the center of tribal languages often has nothing to do with things, objects, but contains a more spiritual sense of the world. Maybe that's why I write poetry, because it's one way I can speak. Writing poetry enables me to speak of things that are more difficult to speak of in "normal" conversations.

I have a feeling that what many American Indian writers are attempting is to bring a new dimension, a new depth to English by returning a spiritual sense to something which has become, as you said, very materialistic and very scientific. German used to be described as the language of science. Today, English is the language of science throughout the world.

I've often wondered why we were all born into this time and this place and why certain things happen the way they do, and sometimes I have to believe it's for those reasons, to learn new ways of looking at things . . . not necessarily new, none of this is really new.

Even without the old language to say some of the things that were there in that old language?

Which is always right there beneath the surface, especially right here in North America, which is an Indian continent.

That ties into something I wanted to ask you, related to the whole question of the half-breed, the person who is of mixed blood. So many contemporary American Indian writers are people who have come from a mixed parentage. Does that mean a separation or isolation or something else?

Well, it means trouble. I've gone through stages with it. I've gone through the stage where I hated everybody who wasn't Indian, which meant part of myself. I went through a really violent kind of stage with that. And then I've gone through in-between stages and I've come to a point where I realize that we are who we are, and I realize that you have to believe that you're special to be born like that because why would anybody give you such a hard burden like that unless they knew you could come through with it, unless with it came some special kind of vision to help you get through it all and to help others through it because you are gifted with a different insight. You see there are more than two sides. It's like this, living is like a diamond or how they cut really fine stones. There are not just two sides but there are so many and they all make up a whole.

No, I've gone through a lot with it. I've talked to Linda Hogan, Leslie, many other people about it, and everybody's probably been through similar stages.

Then there is that point where you come to realize that this is still Indian land, despite people who say, "Well, if you're only half-breed, why do you identify so strongly with Indian ancestry?"

Well, you can't not. I'm sure everybody's thought about it. I've thought about saying, "Hell, no, I don't have a drop of Indian blood in me. I'm not Indian, don't talk to me." Yeah, I've thought of doing that. But then I would be harassed even more. Everybody would come up to me and ask me why am I ashamed. But you just can't do it. And it also means that you have a responsibility being born into that, and I think some of us realize it much more than others. It's given to you, this responsibility, and you can't shake it off, you can't deny it. Otherwise you live in misery.

Barney Bush has spoken about the idea of being tested.

Sure.

Being tested from all kinds of directions at the same time. I especially feel that testing in some of your poems. A tension exists there. It seems to reach a point where it ought to break into violence and yet it doesn't. Why don't they go into violence as some of the poems of the black American writers do? For example, Amiri Baraka's?

I don't know; yet I understand it. There're always effective ways to deal violence. There are ways to temper it. I just read this quote by Gandhi. He's talking about anger and he says, "I have learned through bitter experience the one supreme lesson to conserve my anger, and as heat conserved is transmitted into energy, even so our anger, controlled, can be transmitted into power which can move the world." It seems that the Native American experience has often been bitter. Horrible things have happened over and over. I like to think that bitter experience can be used to move the world, and if we can see that and work toward that instead of killing each other and hurting each other through all the ways that we have done it . . .

The world, not just Indian people, but the world.

Sure, because we're not separate. We're all in this together. It's a realization I came to after dealing with the whole half-breed question. I realized that I'm not separate from myself either, and neither are Indian people separate from the rest of the world. I've talked with James Welch and other writers about being categorized as Indian writers. We're writers, artists. We're human beings and ultimately, when it's all together, there won't be these categories. There won't be these categories of male/female and ultimately we will be accepted for what we are and not divided.

To connect, to celebrate, and also to understand. I think that there's a process of understanding that's going on right now in the United States and throughout the world. In fact, sometimes I think people in Europe are further ahead of many of the people in the United States in terms of listening to what writers such as the American Indian writers are saying and understanding what their messages can mean.

I suppose. I was in Holland a few years ago reading. I remember riding on a train and talking with a woman from Indonesia, and she told about how Indonesians are treated in Holland. I knew they were welcoming the American Indians and tribal people from all over, but they didn't realize that these Indonesians are tribal, too, you know. During the Longest Walk President Carter wouldn't see the people, he said, because he had been out on some human rights mission involving the rest of the world.

Joy, I'd like to ask some questions that deal very specifically with your newest book of poetry, the one that's just about to be published, She Had Some Horses. *Horses occur again and again in your writing. Why?*

I seem them as very sensitive and finely tuned spirits of the psyche. There's this strength running through them.

The idea of strength also seems to fit your images of women. Women in your poems are not like the women I've seen in poems by quite a few Anglo writers. They seem to be different.

I think they're different. I think they teach an androgynous kind of spirit where they are very strong people. They're very strong people, and yet to be strong does not mean to be male, to be strong does not mean to lose femininity, which is what the dominant culture has taught. We're human beings.

I like that. A woman or a man simply being a human being in a poem has not been very possible in the United States in poetry. Instead, the sexes are divided into stereotypes.

It's time to break all the stereotypes. The major principle of this universe, this earth, is polarity. Sometimes I think that it doesn't have to be, but the level that earth is, it is. You have to deal with it. I'm not saying it has to be that way—you have all these wonderful things going on in terms of consciousness. Such a split.

Ironic. It's like the old maxim that there wouldn't be angels without devils.

Or, again, like Gandhi's saying that experiences that anger can turn into a power that can move the world.

You're saying that things which are not properly used have destructive potential but then when they're used in the right way they become creative. Even those things which seem to be curses we can turn into blessings.

You always have to believe you can do that.

Another question about your images or themes . . . Noni Daylight. I've gotten to know and like her in your poems. Who is Noni Daylight, and how did she come to your poems?

In the beginning she became another way for me to speak. She left me and went into one of Barney's poems. I haven't seen her since. [laughter] Which poem was it? It was in his latest book. I remember when Barney showed me that poem, he was staying with me one Christmas and I looked at it and said, "Oh, there she is." She left and I really haven't written any poems about her since. She was a good friend who was there at a time in my life and she's gone on.

When did you start writing poetry?

When I was at the University of New Mexico. Probably right around the time Rainy was born.

So you started relatively late in life—compared to some people.

Yeah, I never had a burning desire to write until rather recently. I always wanted to be an artist. When I was a little kid I was always drawing, and many of my relatives were pretty good artists. My favorite aunt, the one I spoke of earlier, was a very good artist. That's what I always did and it wasn't until much later that I got started, even interested, in writing.

What do you think created that interest?

Reading poetry and hearing that there was such a thing as Indians writing and hearing people read and talk, then writing down my own things.

Who were the people who were your influences at that time?

Simon Ortiz, Leslie Silko, Flannery O'Connor. The black writers have always influenced me, also African writers, 'cause here was another way of seeing language and another way of using it that wasn't white European male.

Seeing that freedom of expression?

Sure. And I always loved James Wright. He was always one of my favorite poets. He has a beautiful sense of America. Pablo

Neruda is also someone whose work I appreciate, learned from.

Neruda speaks about writing a poetry of the impurity of the body, rather than a "pure" poetry. A poetry as broad as the earth is broad, bringing all things into it. I can see that feeling in your work.

Yes, it's there.

What's the landscape of your poems?

The landscape of them? It's between a woman and all the places I've ever been. It's contained in the core of Oklahoma and New Mexico.

Traveling seems to be a really major force in your writing. Movement, continual movement. I think I see a sort of motion through your new book. Is there a structure you had in mind when you put it together?

I had a hard time with this book for a long time. I could not put it together right. So a friend of mine, Brenda Peterson, who is a fine novelist and a very good editor, volunteered. She did an excellent job, and what I like about it is that the first poem in the first section is called "Call It Fear." It was an older poem. And the last section which is only one poem is called "I Give You Back," which has to do with giving back that fear.

The way it's arranged makes the book almost like an exorcism, too.

It is . . .

So it's not just another one of these cases where "poetry makes nothing happen."

No, I don't believe that or I wouldn't do it. I know that it does have effect and it does make things happen.

What does poetry do?

I've had all kinds of experiences that verify how things happen and how certain words or certain things make particular events happen. There's a poem that's in the new manuscript about an eagle who circled over us four times at Salt River Reservation. I wrote the poem for that eagle and took it back and gave it to the people who were there and one of the women took it outside the next morning to read it, and the eagle came back. You know, that kind of thing happens. So I realize writing can help change the world. I'm aware of the power of language which isn't meaningless words. . . . Sound is an extension of all, and sound is spirit, motion.

Yes, sound is spirit.

Everything, anything that anybody says, it does go out and makes change in the world.

What about political poetry? Or do you think of your poetry as nonpolitical?

No, I think it's very political. But, I look at a lot of other people's poems, like June Jordan, Carolyn Forché, Audre Lorde—I love their work. It's very political. Political means great movers. To me, you can define political in a number of ways. But I would hope it was in the sense that it does help move and change consciousness in terms of how different peoples and cultures are seen, evolve.

That's great. Who do you like right now among contemporary writers? I'm not just thinking in terms of the American Indian writers, although maybe we could start with them. Who do you feel are the important people among Native American writers?

Well, I think everybody is. I don't want to exclude.

That makes me think of what someone said to me at the American Writer's Congress. You remember that panel discussion?

I remember that panel.

There were more of us than there were in the audience.

We had a good time.

It was great. But one person came up to me afterward and said they couldn't understand why we all seemed to know each other and like each other.

That's because there's such competition in the literary world. . . . That doesn't mean, however, that there's none of that going on in our community!

Why is there such a sense of community? Even when people get angry at each other or gossip about each other, there's a lot of that.

Oh, I know, I was going to ask you what you heard. [laughter]

Yet there does seem to be a sense of community among the people who are Indian writers today.

I suppose because the struggles are very familiar, places we've all been. It's very familiar and we feel closer. But at the same time I really can't help but think that at some point it will all be this way, the community will be a world community, and not just here.

Do you notice that tendency in contemporary American writing?

Yes, I do. I do more listening than I do reading about what's going on . . . I call it feeling from the air, like airwaves. I see other people opening and turning to more communal things, especially among women.

That's a good point. Could you say a few words about that?

The strongest writing that's going on in the United States today is women's writing. They're tunneling into themselves, into histories and roots. And again, I think maybe that has to do with the polarity of earth. In order to get to those roots, in order to have that vision, you keep going outward to see you have to have that, to be able to go back the other way. You have to have those roots. And it seems like they're recognizing that, whereas other writing doesn't often feel it has a center to work from.

I like the fact that you dedicated your book, partially, to Meridel LeSueur.

She does recognize who she is, what she is from, and there is no separation. You know, she's been going at it a long time, has faced much opposition, and has kept on talking and speaking in such a beautiful and lyrical voice.

F. Scott Fitzgerald said there are no second acts in American lives. But LeSueur's life and writing seems to prove Fitzgerald wrong.

She's really had a lot of influence on me in terms of being a woman who speaks as a woman and has been often criticized for it, and in the past she could not get her books published because she kept to her particular viewpoint and was sympathetic to certain unpopular viewpoints.

And has influenced a lot of other women, too.

Definitely.

To begin writing at a point when most people would say your career is all set. You're a housewife, you're this, you're that, you're something else, you're not a writer. To begin to write at an age when most men have already been writing for ten or fifteen years . . .

Well, I always knew I wanted to do something creative. When I was a kid I always used to draw, paint. I even had pieces at Philbrook Art Center, in a children's art show. I always knew I wanted to be some kind of artist . . . and here I am, writing.

One last question. Your Native American ancestry is Creek. How do you deal with that particular ancestry in your poetry? Does that affect you as it has some other Indian writers?

I've always been Creek. But I was raised in an urban setting and in a broken family . . . It all influenced me. I was born into it and since then I've gone back and I'm very connected to the place, to relatives, and to those stories. They always recognize me. My father who was not always there but his presence always was—certainly the stories about him were!

But you're not artificially going back and, say, pulling Creek words out of a dictionary?

No, I mean that's who I've always been.

Yeah, you don't have to do that. There's not need to prove *that ancestry.*

No, they know who I am. They know my aunt Lois. You could sit down and talk with her, she knew who everybody was and who's related to who, you know, all of them, and they all know who everybody is. They'll say, "Oh, so you're so 'n' so's daughter." And they watch you real close, especially if you have white blood in you. Bad. [laughter] So in a way, I suppose, the whole half-breed thing gives you this incredible responsibility but it also gives you a little bit more freedom than anyone because you have an excuse for your craziness.

That's nice.

Of course, you realize it is because, oh, you're an Indian like Linda says, but it's the white blood that makes you that way. [laughter]

I like that.

And you also always have to have a sense of humor about it all.

Yes, a sense of humor is right. We didn't talk about that, did we?

I remember that one jail in Anchorage. I went in there three times and the place would get more and more packed each time I came in because we would sit around and tell stories and—it was all men—and talk and laugh and they didn't want me to go because nobody allowed them to speak. We would all be crying at the end, and I remember when Henry told the story, yeah, you know, we were just laughing at him and saying, you know, you're full of crap, yet the story was really true. We all knew it was absolutely true and it was so sad that it had to be so funny.

Ancestral Voices
Interview with Bill Moyers

You said this morning that you discovered your language came from some other place and that it was different from the language being spoken around you as you were growing up. What was that place?

I guess you would call it that mythic place—that river ultimately—that is within all of us which is not tapped as often with the general public as it used to be in cultures which had living oral traditions and very vital heroes and heroines. In our time it's tapped by the artists—you could hear it today in the performances as people pulled on that incredibly rich source.

How did you tap it yourself?

I guess painting first got me in touch with it. I have a full-blood Creek grandmother who was a painter and my aunt was a painter. From the time I was a child I always knew there was something very important that I was given to do, and although I didn't always have the words for it, I knew that I was going to be an artist—I would always say, "I'm going to be an artist when I grow up."

As a child, I had a very difficult time speaking—I remember the teachers at school threatening to write my parents because I was not speaking in class, but I was terrified. Painting was a way for me to do what I felt it was given to me to do: I won all the art awards at school, and I had my work on

---

From *The Power of the Word* Series, PBS, 1989.

exhibit from a very young age. After grade school I went to the Institute of American Indian Arts, which at that point it was an all-Indian arts high school.

Do you remember the first time you wrote a poem?

One day in the eighth grade the teacher came in and said, "All right, everyone's got to write a poem." We were dumbfounded—a poem? There was a state anthology she wanted her students to be represented in, so we all wrote poems. Mine was terrible—I don't remember it—but I did get an honorable mention for a story. The next time I consciously remember writing was at Indian school when I wrote acid rock songs for an all-Indian acid rock band in Santa Fe. I hope none of those survive.

That's not a very auspicious beginning for a poet.

It wasn't until I was about twenty-two and a student at the University of New Mexico—I was majoring in painting after starting out in pre-med—that I started listening to poetry and writing my own poetry. It was at that time that I met Simon Ortiz and Leslie Silko and also heard Galway Kinnell read poetry—he was one of the first poets I ever heard, and a great love for poetry evolved from that experience.

You said today that when you write an old Creek Indian enters the room and stands over you.

Yes, that does happen sometimes. I think my muse takes different forms, but I have often felt this presence. Sometimes it seems to be a singular presence and other times it seems to be multiple. I have a very old tie-in, of course, with my father's people—I feel they're behind what I do—but sometimes the presence seems something else entirely. I have a poem called "The Woman Hanging from the Thirteenth Floor Window" that came out of my first trip to Chicago, the first huge city I had ever been in. I went to the Chicago Indian Center which struck me as unusually angular and hard, and in the Indian

Center I came across a rocking chair which was very round, and which actually *shocked* me in its roundness.

Over the next three years this rocking chair would appear at the edge of my vision—different people from the Indian Center appeared in it, and once there were a couple of little girls rocking and laughing and giggling, as little girls will. Another time it was an old man who sat and sang songs to himself in his native language. Finally, this woman came and sat—she had probably gone to Chicago on one of the relocation programs, or maybe her parents had—but she appeared in the rocking chair and she would not let me get up from my typewriter until I wrote the poem. So it's *her* story, and I also consider her a muse of sorts.

Do you ever feel the presence of ancestors? Of grandparents or great-grandparents?

Oh, sure I do. You might think I'm crazy, but I *do* feel the presence of such a world. In fact, I have a new poem about the presence of those other worlds and the ways in which they interact. I have a sense of *all* those worlds as being very, very alive. In the beginning when I was writing poetry, a poem had definite limits—I started out knowing definitely what I wanted to begin and end with, or one particular image that I wanted to stay with. Now I feel that my poems have become travels *into* that other space.

I certainly can see many worlds in your poems, and often contrasting images juxtaposed—horses and jazz, eagles and airplanes, cities and space that just stretches into the universe—I see many different worlds.

That's how it *is*. I don't see time as linear. I don't see things as beginning and ending. A lot of people have a hard time understanding native people and native patience—they wonder why we aren't out marching to accomplish something. There is no question that we have had an incredible history, but I think to understand Indian people and the native mind you have to understand that we experience the world very differently. For us, there is not just *this* world, there's also a layering of others. Time is not divided by minutes and hours, and everything has presence and meaning within this landscape of timelessness.

I love the image of Black Elk, a Sioux boy who talks about the hoop of his nation and the mini-hoops, interconnected and interlocking, moving out in a constantly expanding horizon.

For me the *illusion* is that we're separate. *That's* the illusion. One of my favorite stories lately is of a phone call I had from a friend who was recently made an official of his tribe in the Southwest. He was ecstatic to be home because he had lived out in the world, and now he was taking part in the ceremonies of his people, praying outside in the moonlight on a wonderful night—very dark and very cold so the sky had that icy clarity that lets you see into it forever. Of course they were praying for their people; but what most Americans and most people don't understand is that they were praying not just for their people, but for *everyone*, for *all* people.

The young people today were very touched when you said to them "When you pray, open your whole self." How does someone who is not a native person do that?

There's an incredible relationship of guilt between native people and white Americans. It's an odd relationship. Many white Americans think native people have special spiritual knowledge or know certain tricks. Certainly there are some people who are more in touch with those things than others, but we *all* have prayer. Prayer was *not* just designated to native people, and there are *no* special spiritual qualities designated for native people. Of course, at one point we were *all* tribal people. Europeans were tribal people; all around the world the roots of all human beings were tribal.

But somehow you in particular seem to be in touch with that heritage in a way that is alive right now.

The heritage *is* alive, but I always meet people who think that Indian people are dead. They don't see Indian people even if they are in a roomful of them because Indian people don't look the way they do on TV. Indian people often don't look real because real for many people is Hollywood real. We live in a reality that has been falsely created, and this is especially true for the younger generation. Many people assume that all Indian people lived a long time ago in a certain way and wore certain clothes, so if you don't look like that now, you're not really Indian people; but all cultures change. In our case, the change has certainly been abrupt and shocking, and we *have* had to a struggle to maintain the heritage within that terrible upheaval.

Maybe *all* artists now must struggle to understand the connections between the world of heritage and the present world. Those worlds certainly do converge and maybe poems are points of convergence or, in some sense, paintings of that convergence. Maybe the artist has always worked to find those connections, but I think the struggle is especially important in these difficult times when the illusion of separation among peoples has become so clear.

You said "illusion."

Because I think it *is* an illusion. I think this is more the shadow world than it is the real world.

This world of alienation and of separation is the shadow world?

Yes, but this shadow world is also *very* real. There are many wars going on all over the world and each of them is very real, and the losses people suffer because of them are very real. I don't mean to deny that at all.

And yet there is something underneath that the artist sees?

Yes, but I think artists always have to include what's apparent and real in that vision, even while we're always searching for what makes sense *beyond* this world.

"Searching for" sometimes means "calling up," doesn't it? Your poems carry this marvelous capacity for creating what I didn't know I'd forgotten in images that I haven't thought about in a long time. Memories run all through your poems. I noticed that the students really liked the one you read today called "Remember." What is the relationship of poetry to memory in your own life? What are you remembering?

Especially because I'm a person from a tribe in the United States of America, I feel charged with a responsibility to remember. I suppose *any* poet in *any* tribal situation feels that charge to address the truth which always includes not just the present but the past and the future as well.

Did you hear poems and stories when you were growing up in Oklahoma?

I have to recognize that one of my influences is country and western music. When I was very young my mother often sat at the table with an old typewriter, writing song lyrics for country western songs which she would then send out. Of course I also heard many stories about my family.

Tell me about your family.

I suppose the person who influenced me the most was my aunt Lois Harjo Ball. She was a painter, and I was always amazed by what she could remember. In fact, I've always been amazed at what native people can remember. Native people are from oral cultures—they may be able to read and write, sometimes even in their own language, but the expression of the culture is primarily oral. So they're incredibly gifted in memory and in telling stories.

For example, even though she wasn't there, my aunt Lois Harjo could remember what people were wearing as they walked on the Trail of Tears. She had heard the stories of that terrible walk, and the story of Monahwee who fought against Andrew Jackson in the Redstick War—one of the Creek Wars fought against the move to Oklahoma, but we wound up having to move anyway. Many of the people who fought in that war went down to Florida and became part of the Seminoles, but he was forced to go to Oklahoma. Anyhow, she had been with other older Creek people who, for example, described Monahwee's horse and a little black dog that someone else had, things that you would never find in history books.

This was in the 1950s and they were talking about events over a hundred years ago that had not been written down! Did these stories come down father to son, mother to daughter, right on through the ages, a kind of poetry?

Yes, they *are* a kind of poetry, and I greatly admire the speakers, those who keep the stories alive. My paternal grandfather was a Creek Baptist minister, and although he died long before I was born, I always recognize something of his life in what I am doing. I love the ability to tell a story and to tell it well. Traditionally, wealth was often determined by your gifts in this area—How many songs do you know? How many stories can you tell? And how *well* can you tell them? I think the skills which enabled the retelling of memory were seen as our *true* riches.

What was it like growing up in Oklahoma in the 1950s? Was there still a lot of discrimination and prejudice toward Indian people?

Yes, there was a lot of discrimination toward Indian people. I didn't get much of it because I'm not a full-blood, but people did know about me and I certainly look like one of the breeds around there, so I've had some experiences with prejudice there and out in the world as well. For example, several of us in one of the first all-Indian drama and dance troupes in the United States were walking down the street in LeGrand, Oregon, when people suddenly began to throw rocks and spit at us and abuse us verbally; but other native people have had to deal with that experience almost constantly.

Did you think being born of mixed blood was a curse?

Sure. There were times when I went through a period of really hating myself for being a mixture of both races. I wanted to be either all of one or all of the other because in some ways I think it would have been easier, but at the same time part of my lesson in this life is to recognize myself as a whole person and to recognize the possibility that because of this mixture I have something that no one else has. We each have our own particular gifts, but I've had to take what has been, to me, a symbol of destruction, and turn into creative stuff.

Has poetry helped you do that?

Definitely. Poetry has given me a voice, a way to speak, and it has certainly enriched my vision so that I can see more clearly.

So many of your poems begin with fear and end with love. Does that happen in the course of writing the poem? Is writing the poem itself a process of reconciliation? Or is it a design you're following in your mind, going from fear to love because that's the way you planned it?

I'm aware of being involved with transformation in my work. I spend much of my time with Indian people, and I love my people—I love human beings, period!—but because I've seen a lot of destruction and many of the effects of that destruction—the alcohol, the government programs, and so on—I know that I want to work with all that and encourage the incredible live spirit in my people. I want to have some effect in the world; I want my poetry to be useful in a native context as it traditionally has been. In a native context art was not just something beautiful to put up on the wall and look at; it was created in the context of its *usefulness* for the people.

So what do you hope your poems do?

I hope that on some level they can transform hatred into love. Maybe that's being too idealistic; but I *know* that language is alive and living, so I hope that in some small way my poems *can* transform hatred into love.

Didn't you set out to study medicine?

Sometimes I think there are other paths that we each could have taken, and in my own case I sometimes think there's a part of me that's probably somewhere working as a doctor.

Language has a healing capacity.

It does and I understand that; but I also love *poetry*. I mean I love what the *words* can do. I love the *language*, the *music* that happens. I'm not going at this because I want something in particular to happen; I do it because I love what I can *make* with it.

What can you tell me about the poem called "I Give You Back"? It's such a beautiful poem.

It's a poem that I wrote specifically to get rid of fear, and I've gotten more letters from people about this poem than about any other.

Your own fear?

Yes, my own fear. Sometimes I feel that it's a fear linked up to generations and that we all carry it. I think of my mother and what she lived through in coming out of extreme poverty, and I understand what's been passed on to me and what was passed on to her and so on. Just as there is a love that gets transmitted, there's probably a fear that gets transmitted, too. So when I come up against it, I sometimes feel that it's a fear engendered in *many* of us. What I'm touching on in this poem is a fear or a force that includes generations of warfare, slaughter, and massacre. I'm thinking especially of America.

Did it work for you?

I think it did, and it does. I guess what I'm having to learn is to make fear an ally instead of just an enemy. I'm trying to understand this destructive force and, in some way, to take it into myself. Otherwise, it's always going to be the enemy—if it's out there, it will always be your enemy and it will always be following you around.

Let me ask you a question about poetic construction. In "I Give You Back" you say, "You can't live in my eyes, my ears, my voice / my belly, or in my heart my heart / my heart. . . . my heart." You repeat "my heart" four times. Why?

Well, it mimics the heartbeat.

Oh, sure—Bum, ba-bum, ba-bum.

Yes. I don't know if I did it consciously, but now I can look at it and say, "Well, that's what it does." In fact, you *don't* always know what you're doing.

You really don't?

Not really. You may consciously do some things, including setting up forms, but when you're involved in the original construction of the poem, you're *not* in your left brain—the beginning of the poem comes out of the *right* brain.

Why do horses keep appearing in your poems? They're everywhere, horses of all shapes and sizes.

They just showed up, and they're very much present. I finally linked their appearance to an experience I had when I was still an undergraduate at the University of New Mexico and Puerto del Sol Press, which was down in Las Cruces, was doing my first chapbook. I was driving my little red truck from Albuquerque to Las Cruces to help with the book and then to do a reading, and somewhere halfway between those cities a horse appeared to me.

I could smell the horse and I could see it at the edge of my vision, and this horse was a very old friend, someone I hadn't seen in a long time. This might sound crazy—I don't know any other way to explain it—but *that's* what happened; I had tears running down from my eyes because it was so good to see this horse whom I hadn't seen in years. I notice that for me certain forces seem to take two or three years before they come into being, and it took about that long before the poems with the horses began to emerge. Now I attribute this book to that horse.

Are you comfortable now living in two worlds and also in that world that's blended from the two?

Yes and no. I don't know that I'm ever really comfortable.

Are you still active politically, or has poetry taken your passion?

I think you can be active politically *in* poetry. I feel that I'm doing my work in poetry, although I certainly do still take part and try to be some kind of force in the community partly through my teaching and partly through the talking I do with young Indian people all over the country. I don't think everyone is meant to be out on the front lines, doing grassroots organizing. I think we all contribute as we can.

You can probably reach more people through television, through journalism, through teaching, than you can through poetry. Do you get discouraged because poetry has such a relatively small audience in this country?

That *is* frustrating sometimes, and it's certainly *not* the situation in all other countries. It was very refreshing to go to Amsterdam, for example, and to find that the general population loves poetry. When you go into a little store there you find people who know and love poetry. Here in the United States there is a hunger for poetry, and I think that's one reason why we have the mythology of the rock star and such a drive toward that music among young people.

There is also a hunger for love. I was intrigued this afternoon when you said "Every poem is a love poem." In what sense did you mean that?

Well, love isn't necessarily romantic. Sometimes love is just hardcore front lines; I don't want to say warfare, but it *can* be very gritty.

In what sense is every *poem a love poem?*

You have to be feeling some sort of love to sit down and spend the time involved in the creation of poetry, especially when— as you said—the audience is not as large as it is elsewhere in the world; but I also mean that all poems are love poems in another sense which involves the power of language and the real nature of what a poem is. Ultimately, a poem has an electrical force field which *is* love. In one of my poems, "Day of the Dead," I have a line, "Love changes molecular structure," and that line describes something of what a poem does.

A poem may be about death or destruction or anything else terrible, but I somehow always want it to resolve, and in some manner I want the resolution of that poem to *be* love. When that doesn't happen it makes me nervous. I *do* have to be open for the poem to go its own way, but I think the natural movement of love is an opening, a place that makes connections.

One certainly feels a sort of cosmic energy coming through those openings at times.

You have to be open in that way to write a poem that really works, and I think there's *always* love involved in the act of creation.

Do you give your students any advice about how to read poetry? I myself don't catch all the poems that I hear, and I noticed today that faces of students would be occasionally bewildered, occasionally rapturous as they were not getting it and then getting it.

First of all, it's important to read the poem out loud. Poetry is an oral art—it's *meant* to be spoken and to be read out loud. I have my students memorize at least two poems a semester, which they usually don't like doing, but they come to see why it's important. I've given thought to having everyone memorize a poem a week—for which I'm sure I would not be very popular—but there's such magic in doing that. Then it's important to be willing to let go of your immediate reality and enter the poet's world. You also have to be able to let go of a particular kind of reason because I think poetry often involves a reasoning more akin to dream reason or nonlinear reason.

Dream reason?

What I would call dream reason is a reasoning that I suppose has the shape of a mythic form, a shape that is not particularly logical in terms of Western thought.

Do you wake up in the middle of the night having dreamed and begin a poem or put your dreams down?

I write my dreams down quite often because they tell me a lot. I don't usually say that I dreamed a particular image or sequence of events in a poem, but certainly that sensibility comes through. We spend nearly half our lives in that world, and I think we all draw on that material, whether consciously or not.

You said today you didn't like to talk about "She Had Some Horses." Why is that?

I suppose because in some sense the material in that poem seems to me more unconscious than conscious. People always ask me, "What do the horses *mean*?" and "Who *are* the horses?" I see the horses as different aspects of a personality which are probably within anyone. We *all* have herds of horses, so to speak, and they can be contradictory. Those contradictions are a part of me: "She had some horses she loved. / She had some horses she hated. / These were the same horses." That ending probably comes out of dealing with the contradictory elements in myself, as I feel them. At times it's been warfare, sometimes *open* warfare; but other times, you finally just have to say, "Hey, let's stop this. Let's see what we can do together."

Sometimes mine are a herd of antagonisms thundering right over the cliff!

Yes. I understand how that feels.

Interestingly enough one of my favorites, "Skeleton of Winter," seems different from those you read today. This is one of the first of your poems that I read, and the line I like most is "I am memory alive." Do we even know these voices that are speaking to us?

No, we don't, and I believe there's another whole way of education that can put us in touch with that world which, to me, is immensely rich. I mean, talk about wealth! That world is the source of real wealth, and people are so hungry for those voices and what they have to tell us. I think what Joseph Campbell was showing us in his study of myths is that those voices are who we *are*.

"I am memory alive." That's what you are.

That's what we *all* are.

Warrior Road

Interview with Helen Jaskoski

I'd like to begin our conversation with a poem, perhaps the first poem you read for us at the NEH seminar. The poem for Rainy.

I began the reading with that poem. It's for my daughter. Her name is Rainy Dawn. In Albuquerque, where she was born, rain is very precious, just as it is here [in Tucson]. And so, her name was of course to bring rain. She was born on a hot July afternoon, and this poem is for her. I wrote it for her on her thirteenth birthday:

Rainy Dawn
(for your thirteenth birthday)

I can still close my eyes and open them four floors up looking south and west from the hospital, the approximate direction of Acoma, and farther on to the roofs of the houses of the gods who have learned there are no endings, only beginnings. That day so hot heat danced in waves off bright car tops, we both stood poised at that door from the east, listened for a long time to the sound of our grandmothers' voices, the brushing wind of sacred wings, the rattle of raindrops in dry gourds. I had to participate in the dreaming you into memory, cupped your head in the bowl of my body as ancestors lined up to give you a name made of their dreams cast once more into this stew of precious spirit and flesh. And let you go, as I am letting you go once more in this ceremony of the living, thirteen years later.

From *Melus: The Journal of the Society for the Study of Multi-Ethnic Literature of the United States* 16, no. 1 (Spring 1989–90).

And when you were born I held you wet and unfolding, like a butterfly newly born from the chrysalis of my body. And breathed with you as you breathed your first breath. Then was your promise to take it on like the rest of us, this immense journey, for love, for rain.

I feel the presence of family members in a number of your poems. I'm thinking right now of "Death Is a Woman," about your father.

My father died about four years ago. I'd been very aware since his death that I hadn't written a poem for him. His death was in many ways tragic, he was young, only fifty-four, and never really trusted life enough to live it. Often those are the hardest kinds of poems to write. I guess what triggered me was a short quote from Simone de Beauvoir: "Death is a woman." I knew then that it made sense in terms of my father, because he chased after his death, as if death were the ultimate good time, the gorgeous knockout (probably blonde). He liked to party, and he liked women.

I was thinking about him, about visiting him, and his death, and I wanted to write a poem for him. He died in Oyster Creek, Texas. He had moved down there probably about ten years before his death, and I was the only one in the family that really kept in close touch with him, that crazy Creek from Oklahoma whom I remember tall, wild, and stubborn as— white people called him "Chief." I was out there in Oyster Creek, it was muggy, hot, fire ants were building forts. I knew he was dying; he had asbestosis, or white lung, from working around asbestos in construction work. It's kind of a long-drawn-out process, that disease. I was going to take him home with me to New Mexico, but he refused. He wanted to stay there in his trailer that was slowly eroding from salt air. We were sitting outside, probably about three or four months before he died, and a cardinal flew over. He said, "Well, that means I'm going to die soon." And so I put that into the poem I called "Death Is a Woman."

This is like other poems you've written that seem to have come out of a vivid single picture or instant, that get put together with a very particular image. I'm thinking of the poem about the javelinas . . .

That's the poem titled "Javelina," and I wrote that this summer here in Tucson. I was remembering standing outside at Leslie's place, and looking over to the west for javelinas that were running through the hills there. I saw their shadows. I was thinking javelinas' thoughts, and wondering what they think of what's going on in their territory, their home. That was half the poem, but I knew that there was a piece missing. Late one afternoon I was driving in South Tucson, and I drove by a Circle K minimarket, and I saw a woman standing at a pay phone with a baby on her hip, and it just brought back a sweep of memories. I wanted to stop and give her some money and go over and say, "You know, things are going to work out all right." I felt bad that I didn't. I didn't know what I could do. So it became part of the poem "Javelina," and consequently perhaps *part* of the javelina.

Leslie Silko has been poet and friend and an important influence on your life.

I started writing as an art student at the University of New Mexico. I met her then. She gave me my first electric typewriter, among other things. She gave me a tremendous amount of support and was one of my best critics. And of course, Simon [Ortiz]. They began it for me. I have to always first acknowledge them. And people like Ishmael Reed and the third world writing community were a great support. (Ishmael Reed and I have gotten into a few disagreements, but that's part of family, too.)

Audre Lorde has been a wonderful mentor and friend. Last October, we were walking down one of those streets near Hunter College, in Manhattan, and I recalled how the Dutch stole Manhattan. But as I looked around I understood that when the native people sold Manhattan they knew what they were doing. They had vision, insight. They knew something was going to happen that they didn't want any part of. "Yes, we'll take those beads and trinkets worth only twenty-four dollars in your money. Take it." Yes, they knew what was going to happen.

So the larger community of Black, Asian, Chicano people had an influence on my work. Some of my favorite writers are African. Amos Tutuola is one of my favorites. And I love Chilean writer Pablo Neruda, for that powerful lyric voice he has, and also the commitment he had for his people.

Is that something you are consciously trying to do as well? To write to a wide community, to reach people who are not necessarily members of a literary elite?

I'm not writing to the poetry mafia, or whatever you might call it. I'm writing first of all for myself. I like what I do. I want to write poems that excite me, first of all. But I also write for a larger community, with a sense of who I am and where I came from—that spirit of history.

You've also mentioned Richard Hugo, as another mentor and influence. Has he also contributed to this idea for you of seeking to reach a wide audience, not just an elite?

I wrote "A Winning Hand" for Richard Hugo. He taught at the University of Montana, and he influenced and gave a lot of support to writers like Roberta Hill and Jim Welch. The first time I met him I was teaching at the Institute of American Indian Arts. I was teaching creative writing classes, and he was reading at the University of New Mexico at Albuquerque, so I took my students down. I loaded up my truck with young writers and we went down to a workshop with him. He was wonderful to the students, encouraging them. I respected him for his humanity, along with his poetry.

While we have been talking about influences and audience using this term, "third world," for lack of a better one, I have been reminded that you have sometimes mentioned a visit to Nicaragua.

I've been there three times. The first time I went with a group was in 1983. I went with a group of women, on a fact-finding tour. We spent two days in Honduras and the rest of the time in Nicaragua, mostly around Managua. We traveled to the Honduras border, and talked to many, many people of various ages and backgrounds.

A poem called "Resurrection" came out of that visit. We visited a little town called Estelí. It's a mountain town, and they had an incredible history. At one point they had lost forty, fifty percent of the village from the war. And in that place, the meeting we had was so striking, so painful, and yet filled with so much love. We were invited to speak, to talk to the people in a church. And when we got there the church was packed with people who wanted to talk to us. It was everyone in the community; it wasn't any select group that was picked out by some committee or other. I have to say this about any visit that I've had: I've always been free to walk around and speak to who I want to speak to, people who are both pro and con Sandinista.

Everyone I know who has been to Nicaragua has said the same thing, that a visitor was always free to go and talk to anyone.

This meeting in the church was amazing. There were a lot of questions back and forth. What came up over and over was this: "We all want to get on with our lives. We don't want your country to bomb us, and we're very afraid of Reagan bombing the country." At that time, they were building bomb shelters and the villagers were having drills. We saw those shelters, which were actually just dirt trenches.

Then in the church we broke up into small groups where we talked more intimately. I was sitting with a woman who looked like my friend Marcella Sandoval's mother, who lives up near Chimayo, New Mexico. We all felt the energy—after the trading of stories, and hearing the stories—the power of those stories. Many of them included torture, destruction, torture, destruction, over and over. And stories of survival. Those who had come back after being tortured, those who were able to escape or survive, said their torturers spoke American English. I was reminded of our people here in North America, another version of the same story.

I have also heard other people say the same thing.

That night, there was so much love exchanged, in the form of stories . . . And so, out of that experience came the poem "Resurrection."

And the poem—the whole experience—has to do with language, too, the power of language.

In America language has become so cheap, words have become cheap. People hear the word "Nicaragua." They read it in the news. They hear the word so often that it becomes without meaning, without humanity. It becomes something sold or bought, as with many things in the English language, not symbolic of a viable, ongoing entity.

Language, used a certain way, can turn anything into a commodity.

They forget that Nicaragua is families, people who look like Marcella Sandoval's grandmother, people who are their own relatives. I say my brothers and sisters several times over, husbands, aunts, and uncles of friends of mine.

Do you find that it's difficult to write? When I came back from El Salvador, I found it difficult to express anything literary or poetic. I wrote something that was just a description, a plain factual report of what I had seen and what people had told me. But it seemed as if the events themselves were so powerful that they couldn't be artistically framed in poetry or fiction. When I read Carolyn Forché, for instance, I find that the journalism she writes is much more powerful than her poetry about Central America.

I do like Forché's work, and I like her poetry. But I haven't written a lot of poetry about it. I wanted to write more, I've tried to write more. It is difficult. I don't want to exploit the experience. But I suppose what happens to me is that I get so overwhelmed by those stories. I have to give everything time to take shape in my subconscious. The sheer weight of memory coupled with imagery constructs poems.

Events themselves are so overpowering that any manipulation of language only distorts or weakens the account. Things are almost beyond language, beyond imagining.

That's why I stayed away for a long time from confronting my own history. I'm starting to examine the history of my tribe. I've always known pieces, stories from relatives. But for a long time I stayed away from reading and learning all that I could, because of the weight of that knowing, which means the acknowledgment of destruction.

What you are saying as a writer becoming more connected with history and tradition brings up the question of language. So I wonder: what about translation? Would you consider translating from Muskogee, traditional works, prose or poetry?

Not translating. I want to learn the language, and I'll probably be spending a lot more time in Oklahoma. I intend to learn what I can. I could see translating as an exercise, doing it as a way to learn the language, the truest face of a people. But that's not really what I'm most interested in. I'm an artist, and it's important to me that I create and incorporate that history.

One of the reasons that I ask about translating, and I'm thinking especially about translating poems and songs, is that we hear so many complaints about translations of oral literature, songs and poems and chants and so on. People say that linguists are doing the translating, and so the translated texts are not very poetic.

I'm one of the ones who have complained about that.

But, in fact, not very many Native American poets are translating. You don't have poets like Momaday or Silko or Welch translating from tribal languages the way Dryden or Pope translated from Greek and Latin. So the classics—the tribal classics—don't get translated by the first-rate poets.

I think many poets struggle to find time to write poetry.

I've brought my copy of your book, She Had Some Horses, *and you've signed it with a beautiful inscription. I like the reference to strength; I think it's so important. I sense it in much of what you have written, about people in Nicaragua, about the girl in the phone booth with the baby on her hip, about people who have to find a tremendous amount of strength and courage just to deal with the most basic demands of ordinary life.*

I admire that. I admire that warrior spirit that I have seen in ordinary people. Like Jacqueline Peters, like Anna Mae Pictou Aquash.

That word "warrior" comes in here, and yet you've been emphasizing nurturing and love. How do you see them reconciled?

I believe those so-called womanly traits are traits of the warrior. Vulnerability is one, you know. The word, warrior, it applies to women just as well. I don't see it as exclusive to a male society. Male and female traits are within each human, anyway. I've known some of the greatest warriors in my lifetime. They've stood up in the face of danger, in the face of hopelessness. They've been brave—not in the national headlines, but they've been true to themselves, and who they are, and to their families. Their act of bravery could have been to feed their children, to more than survive.

You mentioned Jacqueline Peters.

Yes. I wrote a poem called "Strange Fruit" about Jacqueline Peters. She was killed by the Ku Klux Klan. I guess what really stunned me more than anything, too, is to understand that lynching still occurs in the United States, a lynching happened in 1981. When I heard about it, it registered shock waves on my consciousness. One morning I was writing, and her story came out, that voice, came out of somewhere into a poem. They hung her in an olive tree in Concord, California. She had been canvassing the neighborhood, trying to get people to start an NAACP chapter in response to the lynching of a twenty-three or twenty-four-year-old black man, Timothy Lee.

This is like the things you were talking about in Nicaragua. Things happen, Americans are doing them, and these facts never get into the national news. You don't read about American torturers, American-accented English-speaking torturers, about a woman lynched in Concord, in the daily paper or on the network news.

People don't know about Jacqueline Peters, unless someone tells her story. I feel that part of what I do as a writer, part of my responsibility, is to be one of those who help people remember. I feel I have a responsibility to keep these stories alive.

So, again, that is both a nurturing thing and an action of courage, keeping that memory alive by nurturing it, caring about it, and also standing up for who you are and who the people are that you write for. We've circled back to the beginning of our conversation, talking about people, family, and how they connect with and through language, poetry.

We began with a poem, and I'd like to end with one.

You've let me pick one, again from In Mad Love and War, *and the one I think fits here is "For Anna Mae Aquash,"[1] a poem about dying, witnessing, and being here for each other.*

For Anna Mae Aquash, Whose Spirit Is Present Here and in the Dappled
        Stars (for we remember the story and must tell it again so we
                    may all live)

Beneath a sky blurred with mist and wind,
                        I am amazed as I watch the violet
heads of crocuses erupt from the stiff earth
                        after dying for a season,
as I have watched my own dark head
                        appear each morning after entering
the next world
            to come back to this one,
                    amazed.
It is the way in the natural world to understand the place
                            the ghost dancers
named
after the heart/breaking destruction.
                    Anna Mae,
                        everything and nothing changes.

You are the shimmering young woman
                    who found her voice,
when you were warned to be silent, or have your body cut away
from you like an elegant weed.
        You are the one whose spirit is present in the dappled stars.
(They prance and lope like colored horses who stay with us
    through the streets of these steely cities. And I have seen them
        nuzzling the frozen bodies of tattered drunks
                        on the corner.)
This morning when the last star is dimming
                    and the buses grind toward
the middle of the city, I know it is ten years since they buried you
    the second time in Lakota, a language that could
                            free you.
I heard about it in Oklahoma, or New Mexico
            how the wind howled and pulled everything down
    in righteous anger.
(It was the women who told me) and we understood wordlessly
the ripe meaning of your murder.
    As I understand ten years later after the slow changing
                    of the seasons
    that we have just begun to touch
        the dazzling whirlwind of our anger,
we have just begun to perceive the amazed world the ghost dancers
entered
        crazily, beautifully.

NOTE

1. Anna Mae Aquash, a young Micmac Indian woman active in
the American Indian Movement (AIM), was apparently murdered
by the FBI in 1976. See *The Life and Death of Anna Mae Aquash* by
Johanna Brand (Toronto: J. Lorimer, 1978).

The Circular Dream

Interview with Laura Coltelli

When did you start writing?

Not until I was about twenty-two, which I've always thought fairly late. Up to that time I was mostly interested in art, especially painting, and majored in it at the University of New Mexico until my last year, when I transferred to the English Department to graduate with a creative-writing major. I went on to get my M.F.A. in creative writing from the University of Iowa.

Why did you shift from being an art major to creative writing?

Because I found that language, through poetry, was taking on more magical qualities than my painting. I could say more when I wrote. Soon it wasn't a choice. Poetry-speaking "called me" in a sense. And I couldn't say no.

Could you speak about going back to your roots, in your poetry, of your Oklahoma land and heritage?

I just finished a poem today. It's about trying to find the way back. But it's a different place, a mythical place. It's a spiritual landscape that Oklahoma is part of—I always see Oklahoma as my mother, my motherland. I am connected psychically;

From Laura Coltelli, *Winged Words: American Indian Writers Speak*, Lincoln: University of Nebraska Press, 1990.

there is a birth cord that connects me. But I don't live there and don't know that I ever will. It's too familiar, and too painful. My son lives there now; he's going to Sequoyah High School, a tribal school that is now managed by the Cherokee tribe.

So my return usually takes place on a mythical level. I mean, I do travel there as often as I can. I've written a literary column for my tribal newspaper, the *Muskogee Nation News,* know my relatives, keep in touch. There are many memories there for me, it's one of my homes.

How much does your Creek heritage affect your work as a poet?

It provides the underlying psychic structure, within which is a wealth of memory. I was not brought up traditionally Creek, was raised on the north side of Tulsa in a neighborhood where there lived many other mixed-blood Indian families. My neighbors were Seminole Indian, Pawnee, other tribes, and white . . . I know when I write there is an old Creek within me that often participates.

You said once, memory is like "a delta in the skin," so you are "memory alive," your poetry stems from memory always at work.

It is Creek, and touches in on the larger tribal continental memory and the larger human memory, global. It's not something I consciously chose; I mean, I am not a full blood, but it was something that chose me, that lives in me, and I cannot deny it. Sometimes I wish I could disappear into the crowds of the city and lose this responsibility, because it is a responsibility. But I can't. I also see memory as not just associated with past history, past events, past stories, but nonlinear, as in future and ongoing history, events, and stories. And it changes.

You see a very close relationship between writing poetry and "digging piles of earth with a stick: smell it, form it." So, does it mean you're still looking for your roots down there?

They're there. That's no question. When I speak of roots I often mean more than what's usually conjectured. I consider the place we all came from, since the very beginning. It's a place I don't yet have a language for. But, on the more mundane level, I did drive around the United States in my car, alone, about three or four summers ago—just to know it better, this beautiful land. And one place that was most important for me to visit was outside a little town in Alabama called Atmore. There is still a settlement of Creeks there, who hung on through the destruction set off by Andrew Jackson's greed. I went there to say hello, and they welcomed me, treated me well. There is a communication beginning between the Oklahoma Creeks and the Alabama Creeks. We [Oklahoma Creeks] still have the language, the dances, ceremonies, which they have lost much of, but then again, nothing has destroyed their memory, which is strong, and which has kept their small enclave alive through these years of the racist South. I was so proud of them, am proud that they have kept the Creekness alive when Jackson meant them to be destroyed.

My family on my father's side was originally from Alabama. They were forced to leave during the time of Removal [1832], which really wasn't that long ago. In fact, my great-great-grandfather, Monahwee, led the Redstick War of the Creeks against Andrew Jackson. Of course, we know what happened, and Monahwee and his family were forced into Oklahoma. Monahwee said he never wanted to see a white face again; from that part of my family we were rebels, and speakers. So what I am doing makes sense in terms of a family memory.

Do you look at writing as a means of survival?

Sure. I have to. On both a personal level and a larger, communal level. I don't believe I would be alive today if it hadn't been for writing. There were times when I was conscious of holding onto a pen and letting the words flow, painful and from the gut, to keep from letting go of it all. Now, this was when I was much younger, and full of self-hatred. Writing helped me give voice to turn around a terrible silence that was killing me. And on a larger level, if we, as Indian people, Indian women, keep silent, then we will disappear, at least in this level of reality. As Audre Lord says, also, "Your silence will not protect you," which has been a quietly unanimous decision it seems, this last century with Indian people.

She Had Some Horses is a kind of circular journey, walking and talking backward. "Call it Fear" is the very first poem and in the last one, "I Give You Back," "the terrible and beautiful fear" comes to an end. Could you elaborate on that?

"Call it Fear" was one of the earliest poems I wrote in that series, and "I Give You Back" one of the last. I didn't consciously set up the structure of the book that way, but maybe unconsciously I did. I want to thank Brenda Peterson, a novelist-editor friend of mine, for her arrangement. I gave her the manuscript when I couldn't get the arrangement right after many, many tries, and it is because of her that it works well. She understood that I meant a circular journey.

In the last section of the same book you see in the horses the coming of a new people. Does it also shape your identity as a woman?

I'm not sure I know what you mean. When I consider a new people, I consider a people whose spiritual selves are obvious. There are no judgments, or prejudices. Sexual identities are not cause for power plays, and we become fully who we are, whether male, female, or any combination. We need this resurrection, it's who we truly are, yet you could be deceived, especially when you look around the world and see the hatred against the female, and notice, too, that all the wars are basically race wars, white people against the darker-skinned ones. But I am especially speaking of a power that would be called women-woman-intuitive. My work is woman-identified. One of the funniest questions I've been asked as a visitor to an Indian-culture class in a university is, by a male student, "Where are the men in your poems?" He was offended because he didn't see himself, not in the form that he looked for. I truly feel there is a new language coming about—look at the work of Meridel LeSueur, Sharon Doubiago, Linda Hogan,

Alice Walker—it's coming from the women. Something has to be turned around.

The moon image is central to your poetry. Moon as wholeness, which speaks of the universe, a circular design again, which speaks also of woman's life. Is that true?

Yes, although she appears less and less in my new poems. I associate the moon with the past, evoking the past, past fears, and so on.

Your personal past?

Anyone's personal past. Now I am looking toward fire, a renewal. But still aware of the dream, in which the moon appears, a constructive kind of dreaming.

What do you mean by constructive?

I mean, consciously understanding that dreamtime is another kind of cohesive reality that we take part in.

A kind of active perception instead of a passive one.

Yes, it's much more active.

Feminism and tribal heritage—can you see any connection?

The world has changed so much. Yes, I'm sure there is a connection, but so much differs from tribe to tribe.

Because some Indian cultures are woman-oriented?

Some are woman-oriented, especially when you consider the earth as woman, like the Pueblo people of the Southwest. But all have changed over the year after much white contact. And values have changed. Many have evolved, or devolved, into male-centered, male-dominated cultures, following the pattern of the dominant Euro-culture that is American, but generally women were, are, recognized as physically, electrically, whatever, more grounded, in tune with the earth, and again, that's a generalization, because there are always exceptions. You will find "grounded" men, also. I still don't feel as if I have answered your question. I know I walk in and out of several worlds everyday. Some overlap, some never will, or at least not as harmoniously. The word "feminism" doesn't carry over to the tribal world, but a concept mirroring similar meanings would. Let's see, what would it then be called—empowerment, some kind of empowerment.

What does it mean, being an American Indian woman in the United States nowadays?

To begin, it certainly means you are a survivor. Indian people make up only about one-half of one percent of the total population of the United States! It means you carry with you a certain unique perception. And again you are dealing with tribal differences, personal differences, and so on. We are not all alike! Yet, I believe there is a common dream, a common thread between us, mostly unspoken.

I don't believe there are any accidents in why people were born where they were, who they were, or are. There are no accidents. So I realize that being born an American Indian woman in this time and place is with a certain reason, a certain purpose. There are seeds of dreams I hold, and responsibility, that go with being born someone, especially a woman of my tribe, who is also part of this invading other culture, and the larger globe. We in this generation, and the next generation, are dealing with a larger world than the people who went before us—that we know of, because who knows what went down many, many, many years ago that no one remembers. We are dealing with a world consciousness, and have begun to see unity, first with many tribes in the United States and North America with the Pan-Indian movement, and now with the tribal people in the rest of the world, Central and South America, Africa, Australian aborigines, and so on. We are not isolated. No one is. What happens here, happens there. But it is on sometimes subtle yet disturbing levels.

Are you active in women's organizations?

Not really. Sometimes I feel I should be, but it isn't my manner. I participate by doing benefit readings, appearances, taking part when it is useful to do so. I know it is important, and groups are more powerful than one person working alone, but I guess there is no one group that I feel strong enough about to be active in, though I actively take part in many.

Are you suspicious? Of what?

I've wondered. Maybe it comes from being a mixed-blood Indian in this world. I mean, I feel connected to others, but many women's groups have a majority of white women and I honestly can feel uncomfortable, or even voiceless sometimes. I've lived in and out of both worlds for a long time and have learned how to speak—those groups just affect others that way—with a voicelessness. It's my problem, something I've learned to get over, am learning to overcome, because I am often the only one to speak for many of us in those situations. Sometimes it gets pretty comical, bizarre. When I was on the National Endowment for the Arts literature panel I was often the spokesperson-representative for Indian people, black people, all minority people, including women's, lesbian, and gay groups. It was rather ridiculous and angering at the same time, for we were all considered outside the mainstream of American literature. And it's not true, for often we are closer to the center.

Noni Daylight appears in some of your poems, persona poems. You said, "It's like she was a good friend." Would you comment on that, on the persona in your poems?

She began some time ago, as a name I gave a real-life woman I couldn't name in a poem. Then she evolved into her own person, took on her own life. And then she left my poems and went into a poem by Barney Bush, a Shawnee poet, and I never saw her again. She never came back!

What about the other stories of women in your poems? Are they true stories?

Yes, always on some level. I'm a writer, I like to make up stories, to add to them, often make them larger. The "I" is not always me, but a way I chose to speak the poem. "The Woman Hanging from the Thirteenth Floor" is written around an imaginary woman. You could call her imaginary. But within that space she is real, also. I made a trip to Chicago, oh, about eight years ago, and one of the places I went to while I was there was the Chicago Indian Center. The center was rather bleak, as there wasn't extra money around to buy things to make the place warm, homelike; there were no curtains, nothing like that, but in one room I noticed a rocking chair. It may have been empty, or there may have been someone in it—the image stayed with me. Perhaps it was because the chair was round, and everything else, all around, was square. So, a few years after that trip, the image stayed with me, and I would see this woman, rocking and rocking, for her life, and she compelled me to write the poem. And I felt her standing behind me, urging me on as I wrote, kept looking behind me. When it first appeared, and during the first readings of the poem others would come up after the reading and say, "You know, I know that woman," or "I knew her," or "I heard the story and have a newspaper clipping of it," and the event always had occurred in a different place. And other women are composites of many women I know, or stories I've heard, probably much like a fiction writer would work.

So you became a kind of storyteller?

In a way, though I am not a good fiction writer, or should I say, have never really tried it, except in terms of screenplays.

You mentioned before you are not only a poet, but you're a scriptwriter for television and film. How does the process work in translating your poetical world from one medium to another?

Screenwriting is definitely related to poetry. You're dealing again with the translation of emotions into images. There's a similar kind of language involved. One goal I have, a life goal in terms of the cinema, is to create a film with a truly tribal vision, viewpoint, in terms of story, camera viewpoints, angles, everything. It hasn't been done, not on the scale I would like to do it.

What do you think of non-Indian critics of your work and of Indian literature in general?

That question could be answered many ways—I mean, there are specific non-Indian critics who get into trying to be Indian, when they don't have to. What I write, what any of us write, or are after, whether we are Indian, Chicano, Laotian, is shimmering language, poetry, the same as anyone else who is writing in whatever language; with whatever sensibilities. Or too often they won't approach the literature at all, won't read it or speak of it because, again, that guilt enters in, or that fear that keeps them from entering any place other than what is most familiar.

As far as the literature goes, I've seen much growth in these last several years, in all of us. We are setting high standards for ourselves, our own standards, mind you, in terms of what is possible with this language, and with what we have come to know as artists of this continent.

What writers are important to you?

I consider first the writers who got me turned on to writing, what writing could do. Because I was rather a late bloomer in this business, I was never turned on by conventional English-language poetry. These writers include Simon Ortiz, Leslie Silko, and many black American writers, like June Jordan, later Audre Lorde and Alice Walker. Also Pablo Neruda, James Wright, Galway Kinnell, and African writers. I love the work of Amos Tutuola, especially *The Palm Wine Drinkard*. And there are many others.

Do you see any changes in your work?

Yes, many. If I didn't see them, didn't see growth, then I wouldn't do it any more. There are leaps between *What Moon Drove Me to This?* and *She Had Some Horses,* and I expect the leap to be huge between *Horses* and this next collection I am working on. I feel like I am just now learning how to write a poem. It has taken me over ten years to get to this point of just beginning.

And what about in terms of technique?

I'm certainly much more involved with process, inner travel, when I write now than even five years ago.

Can you speak a bit more about these new poems?

For one thing they are not so personal. I am in them, for I believe poets have to be inside their poems somewhere, or the poem won't work. But they aren't so personally revealing, and the space has grown larger. The first book was definitely centered in Oklahoma, or New Mexico. Then, in *Horses,* there was much more traveling, and in the new work [*In Mad Love and War*], there is even more traveling into the inner landscape.

So, in comparison with the other books, how could you define this new book?

Oh, it's hard to say—intensity. I would hope it is more powerful, stirring. "We Must Call a Meeting," is one of the newest poems in it. I'll read what I have, but I might change some of it.

"Language identifies the world." You said that the English language is not enough. "It is a male language, not tribal, not spiritual enough."

Yes, I said that. I have learned to love the language, or rather, what the language can express. But I have felt bound by the strictness imposed by its male-centeredness, its emphasis on nouns. So, it's also challenging, as a poet, to use it to express tribal, spiritual language, being. But maybe all poets basically are after that, and sometimes it isn't enough and that's when those boundaries become frustrating.

What do you mean by saying English is not enough, English is a male language?

Again, maybe it would be that way in any language, the sense of somehow being at a loss for words; [that] could always be the poet's dilemma. The ending of a poem, "Bleed-Through," says it: "There are no words, only sounds / that lead us into the darkest nights / where stars burn into ice / where the dead arise again / to walk in shoes of fire."

Since language has an importance of its own in Indian culture, what's the contribution or influence, just in terms of language, to mainstream American literature?

What I think of immediately is the denial, the incredible denial of anything other than that based on the European soul in American literature. Anything else is seen as "foreign," or not consciously integrated into what is called American literature. It could be ethnocentrism backed by a terrible guilt about what happened in this country.

So what's the contribution, just in terms of language, to mainstream American literature?

That's a difficult question, one that will take me many months to consider, because I'm always thinking about what I can add to the language, as someone of this background—dreams, and so on. I consider first a certain lyricism, a land-based language.

The spirit of place?

Yes, the spirit of place recognized, fed, not even paved over, forgotten. Sometimes I feel like specters of forgotten ones roam the literature of some of these American writers who don't understand where they come from, who they are, where they are going. The strongest writers have always been the ones with a well-defined sense of place—I don't mean you have to be a nature writer—I'm thinking of people like Flannery O'Connor.

What about imagery?

Oh sure, imagery. That's definitely part of it.

A new feeling of landscape perhaps.

Or a knowing of that landscape, as something alive with personality, breathing. Alive with names, alive with events, nonlinear. It's not static and that's a very important point. The Western viewpoint has always been one of the land as wilderness, something to be afraid of, and conquered because of the fear.

The so-called wilderness.

Yes, it depends on your viewpoint what wilderness is. For some the city is a wilderness of concrete and steel, made within a labyrinth of mind.

We Must Call a Meeting

I am fragile, a piece of pottery smoked from fire
                                          made of dung,
the design drawn from nightmares. I am an arrow, painted
                                           with lightning
to seek the way to the name of the enemy,
                              but the arrow has now created
its own language
                       It is a language of lizards and storms, and we have
begun to hold conversations
                         long into the night.
                                  I forget to eat.
I don't work. My children are hungry and the animals who live
in the backyard are starving.
                         I begin to draw maps of stars.

The spirits of old and new ancestors perch on my shoulders.
I make prayers of clear stone
                              of feathers from birds
                                        who live closest to the gods.
The voice of the stone is born
                              of a meeting of yellow birds
who circle the ashes of smoldering volcano.
                              The feathers sweep the prayers up
and away.
              I, too, try to fly but get caught in the crossfire of signals
                        and my spirit drops back down to earth.
I am lost; I am looking for you
          who can help me walk this thin line between the breathing
                              and the dead.
You are the curled serpent in the pottery of nightmares.
You are the dreaming animal who paces back and forth in my head.
We must call a meeting.
                        Give me back my language and build a house
inside it.
          A house of madness.
                    A house for the dead who are not dead.
And the spiral of the sky above it.
And the sun
          and the moon.
                    And the stars to guide us called promise.

from *In Mad Love and War*

Also another new poem, called "Transformations," about turn-
ing someone's hatred into love. I tried to actually work that
transformation in the poem.

Transformations

This poem is a letter to tell you that I have smelled the hatred you
have tried to find me with; you would like to destroy me. Bone
splintered in the eye of one you choose to name your enemy won't
make it better for you to see. It could take a thousand years if you
name it that way, but then, to see after all that time, never could
anything be so clear. Memory has many forms. When I think of
early winter I think of a blackbird laughing in the frozen air;
guards a piece of light. (I saw the whole world caught in that sound,

the sun stopped for a moment because of tough belief.) I don't
know what that has to do with what I am trying to tell you except
that I know you can turn a poem into something else. This poem
could be a bear treading the far northern tundra, smelling the air
for sweet alive meat. Or a piece of seaweed stumbling in the sea. Or
a blackbird, laughing. What I mean is that hatred can be turned
into something else, if you have the right words, the right
meanings, buried in that tender place in your heart where the most
precious animals live. Down the street an ambulance has come to
rescue an old man who is slowly losing his life. Not many can see
that he is already becoming the backyard tree he has tended for
years, before he moves on. He is not sad, but compassionate for the
fears moving around him.

That's what I mean to tell you. On the other side of the place you live
stands a dark woman. She has been trying to talk to you for years.
You have called the same name in the middle of a nightmare,
from the center of miracles. She is beautiful.
This is your hatred back. She loves you.

from *In Mad Love and War*

It's a kind of circular design again.

Yes.

*Would you describe your writing process? I understand that you revise
a lot.*

I begin with the seed of an emotion, a place, and then move
from there. It means hours watching the space form in the
place in front of the typewriter, speaking words, listening to
them, watching them form, and be crossed out, on the paper,
and so on, and yes, revision. I no longer see the poem as an
ending point, perhaps more the end of a journey, an often
long journey that can begin years earlier, say with the blur of
the memory of the sun on someone's cheek, a certain smell, an
ache, and will culminate years later in a poem, sifted through
a point, a lake in my heart through which language must
come. That's what I work with, with my students at the univer-
sity, opening that place within them of original language,

which I believe must be in everyone, but not everyone can reach it.

You said before that you were speaking with your students about your work as well?

I can't separate my work, my writing, from who I am, so of course it comes into the classroom with me in one way or another.

Just a piece of paper with a new poem?

Oh no, as part of that space I teach out of, a space of intuition made up of everything I know as well as what I don't know, and I've learned in writing, and in teaching, that it is important to recognize that place, to open yourself, believing.

Landscape and the Place Inside
Interview with Sharyn Stever

I'd like to begin with the topic of travel which reappears in your poems. Just recently you've been to New York, Portland, and Italy. How do you see travel affecting your poetry?

Certainly travel affects my work, as you know, like anything else I do, absolutely anything else I do—such as raising two children, or teaching. And travel these last few years has taken up much time. But for me this urge to move goes back to childhood. I loved cars, pickups. It was a family joke that at the rattle of keys I would be in the backseat ready to go, though we never went very far, to the grocery store, sometimes the lake, around town. It's always stimulating to travel, to meet people, to be in some other place in the world, for perspective. Suddenly I have another viewpoint on the density of life. It's as if I meet myself, in another version, somewhere else. I've also considered it in light of the removal of the Muskogee people from Alabama to Oklahoma. It was a forced walk away from our original homeland. Perhaps that is also why I am always traveling.

That idea of displacing?

Yes, displacement. I've never felt Oklahoma as my only home, for many reasons. Displacement is a spiritual condition. It is not only physical displacement, but displacement of spirit as

From *Hayden's Ferry Review* 6 (Summer 1990).

well. The original stories first occurred in another landscape, the older spirits live there, a particular matrix that feeds us. It's linked up to the heart. But I suppose the heart will always lead you where you are supposed to go, whether it be in Oklahoma, Alabama, or Arizona. The original impulse of those stories pumps your blood. I've had to learn that my home is within me. I can take it everywhere. It's always there.

But did it take you a while to figure that out, to center that within yourself?

Oh, sure.

Was that "figuring out" a conflict?

Definitely. I've watched it take shape in my work, or rather the work take shape around it. You could call the conflict home, that is, a longing for home. But my overall sense of home means something larger than any place nameable here in this land; it's as if this land is of that larger place, a hint as to the larger story, and it makes a spiral. The poem then becomes a home, sometimes with a glimpse, an eye toward the story of origin, or a place for the human understanding of a hummingbird.

I want to narrow the focus here. I notice that many of the travelers in the poems drive. Could you talk about that idea of driving aside from the journey aspect of it, but the fact that they are actually driving to these places? Do you see that as a more tangible connection to the landscape, that sort of mixing of the people and land?

To speak of driving I'd have to acknowledge what an important event it was for me to even have a car of my own. A car represented independence, certain freedom, ensured that I could move, could participate more freely in the world. Of course, for late-twentieth-century Americans it is an assumed right. But I went from an impoverished teenage marriage to single parenthood, and for many years I didn't have a car, nor did I know how to drive. My son was born when I was seventeen, and my daughter when I was twenty-two. Our mode of transportation was walking or the bus. I remember walking with my daughter in a stroller, diapers piled up behind, a basket on my back with dirty clothes, and my son walking alongside carrying the box of detergent. I dreamed about a car and eventually I bought one for $250 from a friend's father at Taos Pueblo and learned to drive it by taking short jaunts around the neighborhood until I was driving everywhere. Of course, there's more to it than a mode of transportation; I was able to move into the landscape and made many trips to visit particular areas, especially the Jemez Mountains where I would regain my sanity. For me driving is a meditation. Time takes on another aspect on the road, especially on long trips. One summer I drove around the country alone, from Santa Fe to Phoenix, to Venice Beach, California, to San Francisco (actually that stretch I had Jane Miller for a companion; we were both fleeing broken hearts) and then on to Seattle, Montana, Minneapolis to visit Meridel LeSueur, to New York City where I pretended I was a taxi driver and got by well on the streets, to Jacksonville, Florida, to the Poarch Band of the Creek Tribe in Alabama, to see my father who was dying in a little coastal town in south Texas and then home, to Santa Fe. That drive again provided me with perspective, sanity, vision. I stood out on the beach at Jacksonville late one afternoon and saw what Columbus and his ships must have looked like as they arrived in the Americas that fateful day some years ago.

What has happened to Noni Daylight—that persona who appears in several of your poems?

She escaped into someone else's poems. Yeah, she went into one of Barney Bush's poems some years ago, and I haven't seen her since.

*I want to ask another question about Noni. In the poem "I Give You Back" (*She Had Some Horses*) there is an implication that Noni is the other half of a twin. I wonder if she represents the fear the speaker in the poem gives back. Or am I reading too much into the poem?*

I didn't write Noni Daylight specifically into that poem, though a part of her certainly is there, as who she is and what she represents is in all of my poetry. The impulse in that poem was to gather up all the wounded: women, the tribe and other tribes, and provoke a healing in the way that sometimes only the power of language can, by facing fear, addressing it, standing up to it, for fear is a real entity.

That brings me to a couple of other questions about language and words. Leslie Silko says, "that each word that one is speaking has a story of its own too. Often the speakers or tellers go into the story of the words they are using to tell one story so that you get stories within stories." This idea parallels the words that recur in your poems. Each word has power and meaning in the individual poems and then, when collected into a group of poems, that power and meaning is integrated, then extended. Two words that recur throughout your books are "crow" and "sun." What do these words mean for you?

It's difficult to answer that now because they mean something different to me now than they did when I wrote those poems. But crow and sun still appear in my work, and I would think their meaning is exploded because my concept of their meaning has deepened with the density of life. Crow represents a kind of renegade, sort of a free spirit, independent, a wise trickster—a speaker of asides in this tricky unraveling, punctuating the drama, keeping track.

The sun . . .

Well, certainly when I think of the sun, I think of the closest representation we have to God, which is the sun, our closest star, a burning magnificence. I don't mean god in terms of a white man, but in terms of the life force within us; the sun comes closest to that—luminous. We carry our own sun within us; it is the heart. And each nucleus of every cell too carries the sun-heart as the cell. In many of the earliest European accounts of native peoples, it is often said that the natives didn't worship a higher diety, rather the sun. What they didn't know was that these native people were respecting and admiring the sun. The sun was understood as the representation of that magnificence, a giant heart.

Many of the poems are populated with figures that fuse parts of the physical and metaphysical landscapes: woman as wind, crow as the sun, or a cliff as a belly. I see this fusing as generating energy and tension in the work. What would you make of that?

Well, I think it's seeing the world as it really is. It has to do with an understanding of the world in which the spiritual realm and the physical realm are not separate but actually the same thing. The physical world is just another vibration, another aspect of the real world. And so I do this consciously and unconsciously in my work, especially in *In Mad Love and War* and the newer stuff. There are many levels operating in our lives, in stories and poems. In some way what I'm trying to do is make that spiritual realm more manifest, obvious.

And that corresponds with what you say in the preface to Secrets from the Center of the world *when you talk about the landscape with a history and then the movements and voices of that landscape— how there's a place inside us that mirrors that landscape. Is that the same sort of connection?*

Yes, the relationship is reciprocal. Language, behavior, the impulse to live probably arises out of the same place as does landscape. We are obviously affecting the landscape, and the land us, though that aspect is least acknowledged in the Western world. The connection is deep, unassuming, powerful, symbiotic.

Can you name that place inside that you talk about?

I don't know if anybody can name it. Can you? [laughter]

I was thinking about that when writing the question.

Yeah—right. Can you name it? [laughter]

What would I call it? Would I call it heart?

It's not just that. It's sort of like a pathway that links the sun and the heart and the hummingbirds. The hummingbirds come from the sun, the hummingbirds and the crows, and it's a place where understanding is sudden and brilliant. And you touch into that, I suppose, when you approach a nearly perfect poem.

So if you're away, say in a different country, just looking at the scenery, do you ever feel that sudden linking happening to you?

Oh, yes. A lot of new work I have makes those direct connections because I think you can find those links everywhere, anywhere.

Is that always surprising to you, when that happens, or have you come to accept it?

I don't accept it. I try not to just accept anything. [laughter] I always look for that surprise, that leap as Robert Bly called it, or that excitement. But yes, it's always a surprise.

I'd like to move to another topic here. Adrienne Rich, in "When We Dead Awaken: Writing as Re-Vision," discusses criticism and revision. She says that "a radical critique of literature feminist in its impulse would take the work first of all as a clue to how we live, how we have been living, how we have been led to imagine ourselves." Could you talk about this idea in relation to the poem "Woman Hanging from the Thirteenth Floor Window?"

It's certainly a poem about women's lives, from the place in which these women (and this particular woman) live in urban Chicago, in poverty, in a racist culture and within that in sometimes beauty and often, despite incredible odds, survival. And to acknowledge these lives, in print, is a radical thing. I never knew literature could be made of my own life as a woman, as a native woman. I find, too, that the poems teach me; they give me words where I had no words. The impulse for that poem came from a visit I had in Chicago, my first visit there in which I went to the Chicago Indian Center to look for other Indian people. The woman in the poem followed me from that place, not in person, but in spirit so to speak. It came about because of a woman's need to speak, to be seen in a cityscape that deemed her invisible; she made her presence known, so I could not deny her or escape her, for to do so was to deny or escape myself. She sat down at the edge of my memory and refused to move. And I wrote the poem. It was a linking together in which we were all recognized, and I wanted recognition for all of us, past the shame, the destruction, the lies.

To extend that a bit, what do you see as the charge for women writers now? That witnessing, but there has been so much written and talked about in the sense that we, in a radical way, must be aggressive and put ourselves forward in that manner to find out who we are and be heard. But I'm not so sure that's exactly the path to take, and I'm not suggesting passivity here.

I think there is another path. I've thought about it often—this world of the artist in the near twenty-first century, the role of the woman artist, and ultimately all artists. As a poet, I feel first of all that a basic responsibility to the craft—to the music. I'm an artist. But there is a difference in being a male artist and being a woman artist that's not just sociological but gets to the biological structure the spirit acts through, though I firmly believe we are all varying degrees of male-female; for some odd reason we need the division of perception in this particular universe. Women perceive through a body which holds the potential for magic; it's a body that can harbor the creation of another and our perception, language, being is filtered through it. That doesn't change in the twenty-first century, though male scientists are monkeying with that process, propelled perhaps by envy. This particular vision gathers together, makes an impulse to pull together. Whereas, though the male is important to the process of procreation, he has to look outside himself for this magic, and it can be a frustrating thing. Men are much more fragile because of this. Women, therefore, have been charged with much more knowing, and therefore have an immense responsibility. We have been fooled too long into believing in a false empowerment of the male over the female, an empowerment that evolved out of fear.

I guess what I'm talking about is the responsibility that we should take. Or should we should *ourselves?*

I don't like any *shoulds*. That's one word I try to eliminate from my vocabulary. At this moment, the world is in a crucial moment; it's a very powerful moment and it could go either way. It doesn't matter whether you're male, female, white, black, native, what country you're from, rich or poor; we're all in it. It's a moment of global awareness and therefore global responsibility. For the first time, we have images of each other, contacts that weren't probable even twenty years ago. For instance, I am friends with a Maori woman writer from New Zealand, in touch with writers from the Americas, from Poland, from Italy. We make a web; we always have; only now it's more visible. There's a photograph I like to keep near my desk, a NASA photo of Earth taken some distance from the globe. It's obvious we're all in this together. I look at it and think of the earth as the nucleus of a larger cell. The differences are not points of division; rather they link the whole. What you see is one fragile, luminescent, tender, little place, or home.

That reminds me of something you say in Secrets from the Center of the World—*"Everything arrives perfectly in time."*

I feel uncomfortable making a pronouncement as to what women or anyone else should be doing with their lives in this century or any other. I suppose what I am trying to say is that we need to be true to ourselves. I think, given the various constructs whether they be social, political, religious, cultural, that women have not been able to be true to themselves. They've been forced to please men, or rather the patriarchy. Or they've tried to beat the patriarchy. And we understand that the patriarchy is out of control. I call it testosterone madness! [laughter] It's out of control; it's destroying everything; it's created characters like Reagan; it's created general nastiness. I know women have been just as deluded as everyone else. If I see anything, I see that delusion, which is seething with denial and self-hate as the biggest block to creativity, to the affirmation of life, which is what creativity is.

Would you connect that denial to fear?

Certainly. It's all in that same big pot. Fear because you're denying the consequences.

When I read She Had Some Horses, *I continually come back to the word "courage." I'm thinking about the women who populate the poems. Could you talk a bit about the idea of courage and how it applies to those women?*

It takes a great deal of courage to be born into this world; probably the ultimate courageous act is to slide into the world helpless, without a voiceable language, except for the grunts, cries, smiles, and whatever else you can muster, into the arms of virtual strangers who may or may not love you. And without memory, though perhaps we enter with access to all memory, then the first cry shuts it off so we can get on with what is at hand. The women in *Horses* are all composites of women I have known throughout my life, from my mother who has waitressed or cooked in truckstops or cafeterias since my childhood, who used to write lyrics at the kitchen table on an old Underwood typewriter. I can still smell the inky ribbons. They were all songs about heartbreak. To struggling Indian students at the University of New Mexico; they were my first writing audience, and I wrote for all of us, for our survival through some desperate and often very humorous times. To the sometimes mythical women who appeared unexpectedly just when they were needed. Courage does not need to be stated. It most importantly is.

Your individual poems and your work as a whole evoke ceremony. Two poems in particular are "Remember" and "She Had Some Horses," the naming, the repetition. Would you talk about the ceremonial aspect of your work?

At the most basic level, we're all involved in ceremony. Every day the sun comes up. And that is one, the basic way of marking ceremony or the act within that circle, the progression of life. "Remember" was written out of a definite acknowledgement of ceremony. And "She Had Some Horses" too. I suppose there's something dealing with repetition which always illicits that sense of ceremony. And probably because in any kind of ceremonial action, ceremonial pronouncements, the repetition always backs up, enforces the power of what you've said. And this is probably where "She Had Some Horses" has its power because you have "She Had Some Horses" repeating and enforcing what's been said, which is what a ceremony does. It's a ritualized acknowledgement.

You've been working on an anthology of native women writers. What sparked your interest in that project?

Well, again my connections have become much broader; the anthology derived from a global consciousness. And it also came out of me being involved with some Canadian native women writers and activists, and talking to them and just being excited about the work they were doing and sharing with them the work that was going on with native women writers (all native writers) in this country. And we've talked and wondered about what's been going on in Latin America. You hear stories about things going on there which sound very similar, especially in South America, that went on here in the last one hundred or two hundred years since the colonization. So it came out of wanting really to find out what those other native writers are up to in this hemisphere. There's not been an anthology done at all like this; no one has done anything like this. I can see why now. I'm starting to realize what I've gotten myself into—a lot of work. I have two grad students working with me who are wonderful, Val Martinez and Patti Blanco, both poets. Still it's an immense project, but I wanted to do it. It did occur to me, since there's been no such anthology like this done, that I should include men. I wanted to create a span for women's voices. When Brian Swann edited *I Tell You Now*, which consists of autobiographies of contemporary Native American writers, he said the men responded right away, but women had to be asked a couple of times and often thought they couldn't do it and were much more reluctant.

Do you think that's cautious or just reluctant?

Well, for myself, I said (I was thirty-five or thirty-six) I'm not ready to write an autobiography. So, I kind of weaseled out of it. I didn't really do that much; I didn't really write an autobiography. But I think for native women it could be a negative thing for someone who, even if she's out of a very traditional society, still doesn't put herself out there. And I don't think that's necessarily a good thing. I think what is important is that we do say what we need to say and do what we need to do whether we've been given permission or not. We need to give ourselves permission to speak.

While we're talking about new projects, I'd like talk about Secrets from the Center of the World *and how you approached that project.*

Well, it was different; it was a collaboration with Stephen Strom. I did it because I love the photographs, and Steve and I worked well together. And that's how I do anything; if it's something that I love, there's something about that that intrigues me; if I'm moved, I'll risk it. But I was introduced to him by a friend of mine, Rain Parrish, a Navajo woman who at that time was a curator at the Wheelwright Museum. He was looking for someone to write the text for the photographs. All I had to do was look at the photographs. What I like about what he does is that he stops time. I guess, that's a cliché; it's obvious a photograph stops time. But he manages to get an immense section of time. He's able to move light years within the photographic plane. I think that's because he's an astronomer. He spends a lot of his life looking through telescopes;

he's investigating the birth of stars. I mean that he has a well-developed sense of awe. And it translates. I mean it's just lovely, the sheer sensuality, the impeccable arrangements and his framing. He had a stack of photographs, and he had worked on arrangements. I wrote several drafts, and the project evolved.

How do you see In Mad Love and War *different from your previous books of poetry?*

Well, I always like to think my vision expands, deepens. Eventually, I might succeed in not needing words; perhaps the perfect poem is wordless. I knew *In Mad Love* belonged in two sections, one section centering on the "Wars," which deals with destruction; the poems take place in Nicaragua, childhood, a bar, and so on. And the other section, "Mad Love," in which there are love poems of resolution and some from pure lust. Basically, many of the poems are prose poems. I am leaning toward storytelling, which leads to my current work, a series of vignette-like pieces tentatively titled, *The Field of Miracles*. In these pieces lyric threatens to overwhelm the story, and sometimes it does.

How do you see the music that you're involved in affecting your work, or does it?

I'm sure that music does affect my work. It always has, not just the last four years or so that I've begun playing saxophone. I've always liked music, especially jazz, the blues. One of my most intense experiences of music: I am standing in the backseat of the car (this is pre–seat belt era), and I am so short I have to tiptoe to see over the seat to my father and mother. The radio is playing a jazz tune, and I enter the sound of the trumpet playing a solo. I become that sound and am conscious of following the melodic line to the origin of music. That might sound odd, and perhaps I'm not getting it right, in words, and even to say it, in words, might destroy the memory of it. But it was something like that. I know it changed my life. Playing music is a very different process than writing. It's not as initially private. I can rewrite, make my mistakes, and feel so clumsy, so inept until I finally get it right, though of course there are moments of epiphany in which I have the graces of the muses. Music is present as it is, and when you play everything is as it is; music is not a metaphor for something else, though it is evocative. Maybe playing music will make me more honest. I'm not saying I've been dishonest, but there is more room for lying within the written word, though less room for it in poetry. A poem demands honesty. What I mean is that in the process of playing music, you are stripped down to pure musical meaning in front of the listener, and I would like that in my work, for I have kept too many secrets. Maybe *Secrets from the Center of the World* marks the beginning. I'm now thirty-eight and realize how much I've held back and often haven't spoken in the manner I've needed to, out of fear, or whatever else, though I have gone wildly. But what do I have to lose anymore? What do I have to lose?

Horses, Poetry, and Music

Interview with Carol H. Grimes

You've been asked a lot about the animal images in your poems, especially about the horses, but you also have a lot of deer. Do you do that consciously because you are representing the Native American experience, or do your poems come to you in visions of these animals?

Well, it's a very intimate experience. The horses are not something I've just set out to include in my poems because I love horses. Certainly I do love horses and there's a history having to do with that lore. But it often happens in the process of poem making that you don't really know what's going on or totally what you're drawing from until much later. That's part of the nature of writing poems; that is, there are certainly things that you're conscious of getting at. With the horses, I realized later that set of poetry or that sequence of poem making was probably set off by a horse that came to me as I was driving once from between Las Cruces, New Mexico, and Albuquerque. A horse appeared to me. It was a horse that I had known from some long ago time. Who knows what that long ago was, but the horse was very present, and I could smell the horse, and the horse was very familiar. It seemed to be someone I knew from long ago, and so I felt I knew the horse well. I was very happy to see it, so happy that tears ran down my cheeks. I realized later, much later, a few years after the book came out, that that's what triggered *She Had Some Horses*, in which horses are the central symbol, the central metaphor.

From *Kalliope: A Journal of Women's Art* 13, no. 2 (1991).

What do you consider, at this stage of your career, your most important poem, the poem that means the most to you, or that brought you to the strength that you have now?

That's interesting, I've never thought about that. If I think of the poem that causes the strongest reaction, or the poem that is most familiar to people, of course, it's "She Had Some Horses," or "I Give You Back," a poem having to do with fear. That one was a turning point. Now "Eagle Poem" for me has become an important poem, as has the poem "Dawn Appears as Butterflies," which is a new piece and which is between prose and poetry. And "The Myth of Blackbirds."

Are those in your new book that just now came out?

"Eagle Poem" is in *Mad Love and War*, but the other two aren't.

Do you consider these new ones somewhat different from "I Give You Back" and "She Had Some Horses"—are you going in a different direction now?

Sure, I think it's an ongoing thing, an ongoing process of discovery. And I hope there is new ground covered, new territory, new psychic splits of space.

About new directions, you said yesterday that the music that you're doing now is a new thing, that you're just starting to include the music performance. Why did you decide to add music to your performance; how would you say that it relates?

Well, I have a really great love of music, and I love the saxophone. One of my earliest memories of what I would call poetry is standing in the back seat of the car and being so small that the top of my head reached the top of the back seat. I had to stand on my tiptoes to look over the seat. There was a jazz band with a trumpet, and I remember very consciously trying to follow that sound and loving the trail that it made and following it to the source of itself, which was undefinable.

You had a visual sense of doing that?

Yes, very visual, a sense even more than visual, of following it with my whole self. I have always loved music, and for me, the art of poetry is not separate from the art of music. There is not such a separation in tribal cultures. It's only in contemporary Western civilization that the arts become distinctly separate.

So in the tribal culture, poetry is music which is poetry, and that whole oral tradition is both music and poetry? One thing that might occur to new audiences of your poetry performances is why you chose to use electronic music.

I guess I never even questioned that. At a workshop Keith Stoutenburg and I did, in which we actually put together a piece right on the spot, somebody asked why we used electronic instruments, because people usually associate acoustic music with poetry. It seemed that at first it offended their idea of how poetry, especially my poetry, could go with music. It's not something I thought of as being so different. I just thought, well, I want to do the music, and here is Keith, and I want to do this with Keith. I have never improvised before, and I had a good time. I struggled with it, and still there's a lot I'm learning, but I loved it, and that's how it happened. I want to add miking and some of the effects of my saxophone, too. I've just been around a lot of jazz musicians, and that's how they play. They play electrically, and that's what I'm used to. So it doesn't offend my sensibility.

In watching your performance last night with some colleagues, we were surprised, and I guess my surprise faded away as soon as everything started. At first it seemed like a rock concert—

Yes, and why not blur the edges?

Yes, why not? We thought it worked very well, but it was hard to hear some of the phrases. I guess that's what you're working on, trying to get an auditory balance. What other direction in music are you planning, or are you going to be doing the sax and the guitar only?

I'm going to add a bass line. I'm going to add a bass player to develop more dimension.

Do you still plan to say the poems, or do you plan to sing them or use more of a chant?

Well, Keith's a wonderful singer, and I might start doing some work with voice, too.

Where did the rain sticks come from?*

The rain stick I have, I think is from the Huichol people in Mexico. Cecilia Vicuña has a rain stick that's from Chile. She said they're from all over the world. There are rain sticks in Indonesia.

How do you see that the rain stick fits into the poetry? Do you just like the sound of it, the naturalness of the sound, or does it evoke for you a certain feeling or image that helps your performance?

I certainly love the sound of it. It's a very meditative kind of effect. I like the dimensions. It reminds me of the sound of the hummingbird. When I think of the sound of the hummingbird, I think of a bird who can fly in between worlds. They say the hummingbird makes the sound you make when you pass between sleeping and dreaming.

You talk a lot about dreaming. It seems as if when you make decisions, when you get inspirations for poems, when you were naming your granddaughter—that the ideas come in a dream. You seem to have blurred the edges between your conscious life and your dream life. In seeing the horse that appeared to you, you were physically awake, but when the horse appeared to you, you recognized it as if it were in a dream. This is pretty normal for you, right? This is how things come to you often?

---

*The rain stick is a long bamboo shaft filled with thousands of tiny shells. As the stick is tilted from end to end, the shells fall inside the shaft, and the echo against the bamboo resembles gentle rainfall.

I take it for granted that that's how the real world is. That's how the real world is, and most of the world understands that. It's a natural state. There's nothing supernatural or unnatural about it. It's how the world proceeds.

Most people work that way, whether they recognize it or not?

Probably. Some more consciously than others.

In your tribal experience, is this way of making decisions, of getting ideas, matter-of-factly discussed?

Yes.

Because it seems quite supernatural to most people. But then one thing that excited me and my students when we heard "She Had Some Horses" was that horses were exactly the image that says what you wanted. The kind of energy you were talking about in the Eastern tradition describes the warrior feeling you have about yourself being a warrior and having strong energy. And some of the energy is horrible, and some of it is unspeakably wonderful, but it's all the same energy.

Right.

And so that helped us cross that bridge ourselves and see that we have horses too, and that they really are horses and that's the way it needed to be expressed.

You can use a similar analogy, if analogy is the right word, between worlds when you talk about sleeping and waking. It's all the same. Although some people are sleepwalking and, because of their training or whatever, they can't wake up. Or it's been called the real and unreal world, but it's reversed. [We both laugh.] You know, according to tradition.

What would you say to a person who is trying to develop as a poet or trying to develop as a true interpreter of poetry—what advice would you give to bridge that gap, to blur those lines? Do you suggest meditation of some kind, or just listening more carefully to yourself and others?

I think listening has a lot to do with it, listening, giving yourself a lot of space, choosing not to stay safely in what you already know, which means searching for a truthfulness. What you already know is often what you're fed, through television and movies. And that's a safe world, the world we already know. I think you have to venture out beyond that, by listening, by learning.

So someone who has a vision like you had, of the horse and these other visions, could be afraid of that kind of inspiration and not listen to it, and so they don't have to consciously. But you're not afraid of it.

Sometimes it's frightening to see. And sometimes you just think you're crazy. I ran into a young man here who has had no affirmation; he hasn't found the community which accepts him as he is. He will, he is working on it, but it's hard.

You and so many other poets have talked about the community that nourishes you and that you go back to for your truth, to say your truth the way you need to. You seem to see the lack of community that the rest of us suffer from. So much of mainstream America looks at the tribal community and says, "Oh, isn't that too bad, those poor Native Americans, they can't even speak English. How can we get them into the mainstream?" As a teacher, that worries me, that attempt to homogenize everybody into the "culture."

They never seem to consider that people may not want to be in the mainstream.

Maybe they should be worried about getting themselves out of the mainstream.

Actually, in the first interactions between settlers and Indians, the leaders had to make laws keeping the settlers from running away to live with the Indians, because they were enticed by that lifestyle, and many were leaving to go live with the Indian people.

I would imagine, especially considering the choice between living in a Puritan society and the Indian life—

Yes, that would be so stifling. I always wondered what those people did in their secret lives, you know, what secrets they had in their bedrooms.

So many things are written about how that energy became perverted, the sadomasochistic literature of the Victorians—

Yes, because that energy *does* become perverted. That's part of what I was trying to do in "Horses," to show that it has to be recognized and acknowledged, I mean it goes back to that Tao symbol, you know, the light and dark curl that make up the circle.

So you have to recognize the shadow in order to be a whole person.

That's right: the sun and the moon, male and female. I know in my own life, dealing with being Indian and white. All of that follows.

Don't you think that blend of Indian and white gives you a unique perspective?

I do now. I used to hate it. I went through a painful process dealing with that whole issue.

Have you lived more in the white society or the tribal society, or was it sort of half and half?

I kind of lived in both, but I was raised mostly in white. But at the same time I lived in a world in which those people came to me, you know, and I felt I was also being raised by my own people. And I certainly have those connections now, and as I get older and live in the tribal community. My community has always been my own people from the time I was young. But it was tribal people in a city, not out in the hills of Oklahoma. There are urban Indian communities, and the tribal connections are still there. They go to the city to get a job and make a living, so a lot of my people are in the city. They'll go back for ceremonies or go home on the weekends.

So you consciously sought that—you had a choice of whether to go wholly living in the white society or—

I don't know whether I had a choice. I mean, I am who I am, and that's who I am. I've felt from the time I was conscious—

So it was never a question of whether to accept one identity or the other?

Right, it was just "This is who I am."

A lot of white people that I know had a strong affinity with Native Americans when they were children. They study Indian crafts in scouting, and they have Indian Guides and Indian Princesses, and we have this sort of mythologized, synthetic culture that we think of as Native American. And I felt that way, too. I've often asked myself what we are looking for that causes us to fantasize like this about Native Americans.

That's a good question, and I think the answer has to do with being born on this land. When you were born in this country, you were born into the mythic structure of native peoples, the history that has gone on, is still ongoing. There is no past, present, and future. The present is of massacres; the present is of ceremonial events, and so on. We walk in and out of them all the time. And the land is part of that, the land. And the earlier people claim those people born on this continent. And I think that's part of what goes on. The problem is, it's not recognized, and then it becomes very distorted in the way that it's expressed, in which there's no connection: there's a Native American that is totally imaginary, that comes out of movies, that comes out of glorification, of the concept of the noble savage or the pure savage. And that's a very dangerous thing. I call it "stereotypos." But also I think there's a longing for who we really are as human beings, which I think is closer to native cultures, in which respect of all peoples is inherent in those instructions which everyone is given. Ultimately, all people are tribal. Certainly there are cultural differences, tribal differences and so on, but across the line, I think there is a certain basic code which has to do with respect for all life. I think that's part of the attraction, that what people are doing is recognizing somebody that they *are*. That's been disposed of in the system because it can't be bought and sold.

One of the things that my high school students talked about was an interest in investigating their own tribal heritage from the Celtic peoples, which many of them were descended from in the British Isles. I hope that, through seeing you rejoice in your tribal heritage, they will be able to get in touch with theirs, however far removed it may be.

I think it's important for them to know that. There was such a massacre of the tribal self in Europe's history. Where did that come from, and why were they doing it, and who were these people that wanted to destroy humanness?

There are so many parallels between the Native American plight and that of the Celtic peoples of Britain, who had to flee the Teutonic invasions, and ended up in Wales and Cornwall and Ireland, and in many ways, they are still fighting over there. It's a race war, essentially.

Yes, it is; that's what all war is, is race war.

Do you think so?

Yes, and there are no winners in it, never any winners.

Yes, the victors actually lose more than the victims.

That's because of the illusion. The world has this huge illusion that we're fighting. There's a web cast over the eyes of the Western world.

Why do we have that illusion, and where did that illusion come from?

And why do we accept it, because obviously we are born into that illusion and we accept it. The outcome is separation, separation between people, separation between the arts, so that you can't have poetry and music together. People say, "Well, what is this," or "This doesn't follow convention." I went through some feelings. I mean, I got over it, but feelings of being diminished, or as if what I did didn't matter as much to the poetry establishment because, first of all, I'm an Indian poet and because I rely, sometimes directly and sometimes not so directly, on the oral tradition. Quincy [Troupe] was voicing the same thing earlier, about his work not being valued as much because it comes out of the oral tradition. And I noticed in this world, and even at times in this conference, that that happens, that those poets out of that tradition are not valued as much.

You're not treated as if you're a "real poet," is that it?

Sometimes. Of course, you know, I'm going to do what I'm going to do anyway, but that's the sense; that's what you have to fight with in this system. There is not as much value in the oral tradition, or in things not of England or the English literary written tradition. If you don't have the English literary tradition informing the structure of your poetry or informing the structure of your lines, then, you know, you are not a poet. And people will say, of course, there is room for all kinds of poetry, but when it comes down to recognition by those people, they won't recognize other types.

It's a different category, kind of; it's shunted off as a special category.

And it pisses me off. I like what Quincy was saying, that he's neutral, that he includes all people. I do that, too, and yet I get angry because they exclude. They will say something, and then they exclude. They'll say they include, but then there's an exclusion. But I don't want to be negative, I don't want to go on about that, because it gives them power. I would rather celebrate our own new literary tradition, a combination of oral and written, a new movement.

Do you see this as a strong new movement in poetry then?

Oh, yes, and I think it will add depth and variety to poetry that has not been there before. Yes, I feel that it is definitely going in that direction.

The Spectrum of Other Languages

Interview with Bill Aull, James McGowan,
Bruce Morgan, Fay Rouseff-Baker, and
Cai Fitzgerald

In a number of poems in your collection In Mad Love and War, *there seems to be almost a hostility toward language or a frustration with the limitations of language, especially the written English language, as though alphabetic language were inadequate for the job of discovering truth. We're thinking of such poems as "Resurrection," "Deer Dancer," "Eagle Poem," and "We Must Call a Meeting." How does the limitation of language frustrate you?*

My frustration with the language, particularly the English language, stems from anger with the colonization process in which the English language was a vicious tool. The colonizers knew what they were doing when they tried to destroy tribal languages, and which, infuriatingly, they were successful at in many instances. Language is culture, a resonant life form itself that acts on the people and the people on it. The worldview, values, relationships of all kinds—everything, in fact, is addressed in and through a language. I'm always aware of the spectrum of other languages and modes of expression, including, for instance, cloud language, cricket singing talk, and the melodic whir of hummingbirds.

I believe that written language was, in many ways, a deevolution of the communication process. You lose human

From *Tamaqua* 3, no. 1 (Spring 1992).

contact, context of time and place, and a sense of relationship. With written communication, you gain the ability to lie more easily. There is separation between the speaker and the reader/listener. There is less accountability. Of course, both oral and written systems can enrich each other. As a poet, I appreciate the written word, what I am able to do and see within the system of written language, and I never forget that the language, even English, was first oral. Oral traditions provide the underlying matrix for all languages except—and I'm just guessing here—manufactured computer languages.

Because of what the English and Spanish languages represent in this context, what types of resurgence, if any, are occurring in tribal languages? Other than as a cultural curiosity, as in the Irish language revival in Ireland earlier this century, what future roles would tribal language resurgence serve?

Tribal languages are currently at high value I think because of the possibility of their loss, their diminishment. Yet worlds of knowledge are enclosed in them, knowledge that should be valued. In my own tribe, about fifty percent of the people speak Muskogee. Because of the influence of television, movies, and the video rental phenomenon, the younger generation is losing the language. There have been efforts, especially by those in my generation, to learn the language, to speak it to the children. I don't speak it, but because I have spent most of my life in the Southwest, I've learned some of the Navajo language. I was heartened to see that Roseann Willink, who was my Navajo instructor, as well as friends like Ron Kinsel from Lukachukai, is teaching a class next semester at the University of New Mexico in creative writing in the Navajo language. That's the next move, to create in the language. It is then revitalized, renewed.

As a follow-up to the above questions, you are also a musician, primarily a jazz musician. In the poem "Bird," one line reads: "All poets / understand the final uselessness of words." In some ways, this again tries to speak of communication media that are more primal than human language, in the sense that "All art aspires to be music." What aspects of yourself are addressed through language in your poetic art, and what aspects of yourself are addressed through the saxophone in your musical art?

First of all, I don't consider myself a musician yet. I've been playing about six years. I've studied basically classical—I should say, *European* classical, for classical doesn't only apply to things European—and am learning jazz, classical, and otherwise. I will eventually be a musician, but playing a few years does not make one a musician. Just as writing for years doesn't particularly make one a poet. There's more to it. It has to do with devotion to the craft, your mind-heart focused on what makes music, or poetry, for that matter. Both arts, or all art, has to do with thinking about god, and I don't mean the self-righteous, racist, sexist God that was taught to me to hate and fear myself in Sunday school in Tulsa, I mean that-which-is-everything-inspired-and-headed-toward-the-sun. Or more clearly, all art has to do with thinking about acting as god, the creator-who-creates, because that's what god is.

I don't really separate the self who practices the art of saxophone from the self who writes poetry. But I do feel that I initially felt closer to jazz than I ever did to any of the poetry I first read, poetry in which I had to change myself in order to enter the poem. And then there was the language itself. Granted, the poetry had power and changed me, transformed me, but there was always that extra step, a kind of decompression chamber I had to walk through. Music doesn't have the added boundary of words. I have an essay in which I speak about this connection. I'll read a section from it:

> Once I was so small I could barely peer over the top of the back seat of the Cadillac; I wanted to see everything. Around that time I acquired language, or even before that time something happened that changed everything. My concept of language, of what was possible with sound waves was changed by this revelatory moment. It changed even the way I looked at the sun. This small silvery piece of time probably escaped notice of most travelers in that mundane Tulsa afternoon as we

drove through town not far from the Arkansas River, lazing through blood-covered lands. I don't know where we were going, or where we had been, but I knew the sun was boiling the asphalt (though I didn't know the words *boiling* or *asphalt*), the car windows were open (Indian air-conditioning, we call it) as I stood on tiptoes on the floorboard behind my father, a handsome god who smelled of Old Spice, whose slick black hair was always impeccably groomed, who was driving his then small family in his perfectly waxed black car. The radio was on. I loved the radio, jukeboxes, or any magic box containing music. I wonder now what signalled this moment so similar to cosmic consciousness for it could have been any place at any time. I became aware of the line the jazz trumpeter was playing. I didn't know the words *jazz* or *trumpet* or the concepts. I don't know yet how to say it, with what sounds or words, but in that confluence of hot southern afternoon, in the breeze of aftershave and humidity, I followed that sound to the beginning, to the place of birth of music, of that particular line . . . I grieved my parents' failings, my own life which I saw stretched the length of that horn line. I believe then is when I also understood the failings of language, before I could speak.

You seem to be quite comfortable in collaborative work, with photographer Stephen Strom in your latest book Secrets from the Center of the World, *with jazz groups, with film. What does collaborating with other artists do for you?*

I think I first learned about collaborative work when I began working with screenplays. The first screenplay writing job I got was for Silvercloud Video Productions in Tuscon, Arizona. I'd never written a screenplay before but when John Crouch called up and asked me if I could, and I was living on what money I could make as an artist-in-residence—at most, two to four weeks a year—and whatever readings I could get, which weren't many ten years ago, and I was the sole support of my two children, I said, "Yes, of course I can." Wouldn't you? I quickly found a screenplay to learn from, then went to work.

I had to consult with the White Mountain Apache Cultural Arts Board, which was made up of several members of the community. They all had differing viewpoints, imagined different stories. Within the group were parties from opposing political and familial factions. I had to satisfy all of them. That began my education in collaboration of sorts. I also worked with a panel of advisors, and then the producer, the director, and most importantly here, Henry Greenberg, a screenwriter from California who taught me about screen writing. Because of my lack of experience, the NEH, who funded the project, insisted that Silvercloud hire a senior writer to work with me. It could have been a disaster, but Henry taught me well. It was difficult to let go of the story, let it have a life of its own, a story I breathed life into on paper, but diffused by the other collaborators: the board, the director, the producer, the tribal chairman, the storytellers of the tribe. Poetry writing is so much different. Each poem may contain a myriad of memories, but it is generated and completed in a much more solitary process.

The Strom photographic project was different than screenwriting, but something came together that would never have happened if the book was Steve's work alone, or mine alone. I like what can happen when you bounce off another sensibility. In music, collaboration is crucial. Overall, what you create is much larger than anything you can do on your own.

In jazz, there is not much of a tradition of female saxophone players. How did you come to choose the saxophone as your primary jazz instrument?

I chose the saxophone because it sounds close to the human voice. The oboe comes close, as does the cello—instruments I'd also like to play. I got started playing in Denver when I borrowed a tenor sax and got a few lessons from a fine player there, Laura Newman. Then I bought my first sax, a King Super, a brassy horn that taught me to go for it, to not hold back. Then I sold it, bought a Mark VII Selmer, a rather bulky horn that never quite seemed to fit. My next horn I'm in love with, a Selmer Super Action 80. She has a sweet tone, just a beautiful horn. I almost forgot my soprano sax which I acquired between the Mark VII and my last tenor. Another sweet horn.

No, there hasn't been much of a tradition of female saxo-
phonists. That's probably because of the expense and time
involved. Poetry you can write with pencil on the back of a
grocery bag. A horn requires money, and then people to play
with. Women were discouraged from most instruments. I
played clarinet one semester in junior high, and a couple
years before that, with—and I can't quite believe this—a stash
of only two reeds in all that time! I didn't have private lessons,
didn't know the ins and outs of reeds. I quit for two reasons.
One, most of band practice was taken up with disciplining the
trumpet players, who were always roughhousing—they're still
like that. And two, the band director asked for someone to
play alto sax. I was the first to raise my hand and was turned
down because I was a girl! It takes more concentrated air to
play a flute, the instrument most girls played in junior high
band! But women managed to play throughout history. I
think of the famous and successful women's big band from
the thirties and forties, the International Sweethearts of
Rhythm . . . by the way, I love Big Band music, especially
Count Basie.

*Jazz allusions abound in your poetry, some more apparent—Parker,
Holiday, Nat Cole—some less so—"Chief" Joe Moore, whom we do
not know. How does American jazz fit into the Native American
tradition of music as medicine and as communal celebration?*

First, "Chief" Joe Moore was an uncle of a friend of mine. He
was a fine jazz trombonist who left the reservation of the
Tohono O'odam people in southern Arizona to play in New
York City. He was a contemporary of the International Sweet-
hearts of Rhythm. I've always had mixed feeling about the
"Chief" part of his name. That was acquired later, when he
left the reservation, by non-Indians who usually nicknamed
any Indian man "chief." I remember white people calling my
father by that name, as if he didn't have a real name.
    As for my connections with jazz, it's an honest predilection.
The creation of jazz paralleled my own genesis in this world.
Jazz was born via West Africa, mixed with parlor music of
Europe, then the last stop was by way of Muskogee country.

My Muskogee people interacted with African people. There was intermarriage, interchange. My blood is a mixture of all this, just as the music is, though the music is predominantly African.

Many of your poems contain references to African American culture, mainly through musical figures—the aforementioned Parker, Holiday, and Nat Cole—but also to other figures and events—the lynchings of Jacqueline Peters and Timothy Lee. How does the wider historical relationship of African Americans in the European-dominated culture of America inform your work?

I never realized how many African American references I had until you pointed them out. I often think in "tribal" terms, though tribal is tribal specific in those peoples who haven't had their names and tribes destroyed by acculturation and genocide. I know the first poetry I heard in this country that I identified with after Native American poetry was the poetry of African Americans, which I had to search out for the most part because it wasn't part of the curriculum at any level. I was deeply moved. Many of my most important dreams have taken place in West Africa, a place I've never been in the here and now. Recently, I understood why. A few months ago, I was given photographs of my great-grand-parents, Katie Monahwee and Henry Marsey Harjo. I always wondered why the particular silence in my family concerning Marsey, someone I've always felt particularly close to even though he died long before my birth. When I saw the photograph, I understood why the silence. He is at least half African. My relatives prized light skin. Though there was and is intermarriage, racism against African Americans is—I hate to say this, but it's true—prevalent among many tribal members. Racism is usually in reference to white versus nonwhite relationships, but it's alive among nonwhite groups. It's something that needs to be addressed because it's killing all of us.

As someone who continually shifts between the Native culture and the dominant European-centered culture, the dual identity dilemma that results must present any number of paradoxes and difficulties, some of which seem to be represented in the personae of some of your poems: "Song for the Deer and Myself to Return On" seems to address the fragile relationship between the contemporary native poet and her tribal homeland and poetic traditions; in "Autobiography," the persona implies that she has distanced herself from tribal traditions but still feels encroached upon by them and will "carry them with me / In the Spring, I feel my blood"; in "Grace," there seems to be a need for "something larger than the memory of a dispossessed people." How would you address this apparent dilemma?

I disagree with you. The personae in my poems don't have an ambivalence about tribal culture. In "Song for the Deer and Myself to Return On," the tribal homeland is powerful and deep. And lives. The fact that I can write a poem and find my way there emphasizes that relationship between the speaker and the place. In "Autobiography," I carry my tribal past with me, "the same as this body carries the heart as a drum." And in "Grace," the larger memory is the memory of ourselves as we were before destruction as we survive. I learned a long time ago, after much difficulty and near suicide, that I would not allow the duality of blood and cultures to destroy me. I believe the values stressed in my tribal culture are closer to what it means to be a human being. If I can leave this life and have people say, "She was a fine human being," then I have accomplished something. This racial-identity split is another device by the colonizer to destroy us.

How important has the Native American poetic tradition been to you? In some of your poems—"Original Memory," "Day of the Dead," "A Winning Hand," among others—it appears there was a fusion of a number of different writing elements, as though the most appropriate way to be true to the Native American poetic tradition, when rendered into English, is in the flexibility of prose poetry as opposed to, say, the line break method of European prosody. Do such fusions present technical problems for you?

They don't present technical problems for me, but I think they may for someone who prefers or is more comfortable with European prosody. My writing technique is a fusion, much the way jazz is a fusion. I could see myself inside jazz much more vividly than I could see myself writing a poem. That changed, but I've had to make poetry something that fused the various systems of communication. As far as Native American influences are concerned, Native American poetry was scarce when I began writing. I read Scott Momaday's *House Made of Dawn*, which astounded me with its music, Leslie Silko, who was a young writer then, Simon Ortiz, and the writing of the Institute of American Indian Arts poets when I was a high school student there.

One of the more pleasing developments in native writing in recent years has been the emergence of Louis Littlecoon Oliver who, unfortunately, has recently died. Could you talk a bit about his influence, as well as such nineteenth-century poets as Alexander Posey and John Milton Oskison, whose works often allude to people named Harjo?

I won't speak much to Posey and Oskison, although I will say that Alexander Posey is a distant cousin through the people on my father's side of the family, via his grandmother Katie Monahwee. Louis Oliver, a fine Muskogee poet whom I already miss terribly, is the link between the nineteenth-century "Creek" poet and the twentieth-century Muskogee Creek poet. I first met him around 1980 in Tahlequah, Oklahoma, when he attended a workshop on writing that I gave for mostly Cherokee and Creek students at the Flaming Rainbow University—yes, that's the real name, and it was legitimate. Louis was probably the oldest student there, about seventy years old then. He came up to me after my talk and showed me his notebooks. His poems were still the romantic and metered tradition to which Posey belonged. I think I was his first link to a world of poetry outside of books, an active late-twentieth-century tradition in which native poets were performing around the country, writing and reading to both native and predominantly academic audiences, in contact with each other as well as other writers. Soon after he met Carroll Arnett, Joseph Bruchac, and Barney Bush. His writing changed and became a very powerful part of the wave of contemporary Native American poets. I loved him dearly, as we all did. We especially appreciated his very Indian humor, his "sexiness"—I'm saying that for Louis; he'd be thrilled to see that in print! When I say "sexiness," I mean the power that comes with staying more than alive for all of your life.

In your foreword to In Mad Love and War, *you mention the importance of affirming the erotic self through poetry. As a writer, what do you think is the barrier to being honest about the erotic self? Does eroticism present political problems? Cultural difficulties? Religious?*

This is a large question. I'll refer readers to Audre Lorde's groundbreaking essay, "The Uses of the Erotic," which I refer to in that forward. The barrier to honestly regarding the erotic in this country is due in part to the puritanical roots of the original European immigrants. This provides the basis of the dominant culture. The body is to be denied, separated from heart, mind, spirit, a vehicle for the devil, if you will. That is what led to the consumer society. You have to fill up the emptiness of the hole left when there is a separation. An abyss is created within the individual and also within limited cultural expression within such a society. It's what's destroying the earth now. When the body-spirit-mind-emotions-soul are an integrated whole, then a true relationship is experienced in both the inside and outside worlds. I believe this is what Lorde explains in her essay. To be "in the erotic," so to speak, is to be alive. Yes, eroticism presents political problems, cultural difficulties, religious problems because the dominant culture can't function with a society of alive people. I don't equate eroticism with a particular sexuality.

In contemporary Native American writing, the effect of urban society, often disrupting and disorienting, has become a major theme, with resolution coming through reassertion of traditional tribal identity and values. How is this reflected in your poetry?

Probably each poem or story I write deals with this very question. To write, the act of writing, of witnessing means taking part in the healing of the people. You have to recognize that a few hundred years ago, aboriginal peoples were one hundred percent of the population of this continent. Now, we're one-half of one percent of the total population! Now why wouldn't native writers write about the disruption and disorientation? And, of course, the resolution is through reassertion of tribal self. To become part of the mainstream white culture is impossible, especially when one is dark skinned. You are never let in. Many of our people kill themselves trying to become part of that system. So do Euro-Americans. That system is killing everyone. The writer has to turn to that which is nourishing, has to make sense of a senseless history. That's the trick. Leslie Silko does it probably better than anyone. I believe it's reflected in my poetry in many ways. In the poem, "She Had Some Horses," for instance. The loved and hated are joined, are the same one. Maybe that's not true, but in the poem it's true.

Horse imagery is abundant in your poetry, most notably in She Had Some Horses, *of course. How do you conceive of the horse— personally, poetically, mythically?*

I don't like to explain what I do. In fact, I can become quite evasive. Even looking back over this interview, I see I take many evasive actions. Part of that is because I feel a sense of privacy about the act of poetry itself. I feel this especially about the horses. I have a kinship with horses that is beyond explanation. No, I'm not actively involved in raising horses, living with them, yet they are a presence beyond any corral I could construct for the keeping of horses. You ask how I conceived of the horse. . . . Maybe, the horse conceived of me. This world is an interactive world. That's all I want to say.

Recently, there has been extensive discussion in academic circles regarding the teaching of Native American literature as a part of literature survey courses to "illuminate the classics in a new way," as opposed to having Native American literature kept in separate literature classes. What are your feelings about redesigning curricula?

The need for redesigning curricula is long overdue. The whole education system needs rehauling. What values are taught? What skills for being a human being? For the most part, I find the current system terribly shortsighted. For centuries, the system has assumed one authoritative point of view, that of the white male. Anything else is threatening to the system. While there's a move toward multicultural education, there is a tremendous backlash. Why is enriching the curriculum so threatening? Because knowledge is power. What will people do when they find out they've been lied to?

Since 1992 has been declared the Year of the Indigenous People, do you see the probable high visibility of Native Americans as an opportunity or vehicle for native artists to be discovered, or rediscovered, by readers throughout the United States and abroad? What writers do you feel need wider recognition, both past and present?

I'm already tired of hearing about this madman Columbus and discovery. Yet, this quincentenary is important because crucial attention is being paid to the indigenous peoples of this america. I say there never was an "encounter." To have an encounter would be quite a groundbreaking event! That would require Euro-Americans and Europeans to meet native peoples with respect. I don't know that it's ever been done. There was always a hidden agenda, a hierarchy in which the lives of native peoples were counted as worthless, as were the cultures. What a tremendous loss for everyone!

There are many writers who deserve wider recognition. I've always felt Leslie Silko, who has quite a wide recognition, deserves more. I hesitate to name others because I invariably leave out somebody important, but a short list would include: Wendy Rose, Linda Hogan, Greg Sarris, Elizabeth Woody, Janice Gould, Roberta Hill Whiteman, Ray Young Bear, Felipe Molina. The writing of native peoples and the oral literatures overall deserve wider recognition. Most people in this country don't even know there are native writers. I think they stay away because they don't want to be reminded of the holocaust, something they deny in their daily lives. It's the story the land, the animals, and the people will go on telling.

In Love and War and Music

Interview with Marilyn Kallet

What were your beginnings as a writer?

I could look at this in a couple of ways. One is to look at the myths and stories of the people who formed in the place where I entered the world. . . . Another way is to look at when I first consciously called myself a writer. I started writing poetry when I was pretty old, actually—I was about twenty-two. I committed to poetry the day I went in to my painting teacher who mentored me and expected a fine career in painting for me, and told him I was switching my major to poetry. I made the decision to learn what poetry could teach me. It was a painful choice. I come from a family of Muskogee painters. My grandmother and my great-aunt both got their B.F.A.'s in art in the early 1900s. And from the time I was very small you could always find me drawing, whether it was in the dirt or on paper. That was one thing that made me happy. . . . I always said that when I grow up I am going to be a painter, I am going to be an artist. Then I made the decision to work with words and the power of words, to work with language, yet I approach the art as a visual artist. From childhood my perceptions were through the eye of a painter. I feel any writer serves many aspects of culture, including language, but you also serve history, you serve the mythic structure that you're part of, the people, the earth, and so on—and none of these are separate.

From *Kenyon Review* 9, no. 3 (Summer 1993).

It seems like almost any question we ask about your writing, about your cultural background, is going to lead us in the same paths of discussion about your family life, your tribal life, and your life as a writer.

Well, they are not separate, really. Though the way I've come to things is very different from say, Beth Cuthand, who is a Cree writer from Saskatchewan, or Leslie Silko from Laguna. There's a tendency in this country to find one writer of a particular ethnicity and expect her to speak for everyone and expect her experience to be representative of all native women and all native people. My experience is very different from Silko's and Cuthand's, although it's similar in the sense of a generational thing, of certain influences on us and influences we have on each other. But my experience has been predominantly urban. I did not grow up on a reservation—we don't even have a reservation. There are more rural areas where the people are. I'm not a full-blood, and yet I am a full member of my (Muskogee) tribe, and I have been a full member of my tribe since my birth into the tribe. I find some people have preconceived ideas—I was talking to this guy on the plane and he says, "Well, you don't fit my idea of an Indian." What does that mean? I think for most people in this country, it means to be a Hollywood version of a Plains tribe, as falsely imagined 100 or 150 years ago. Most people in this country have learned all they know about Indian people from movies and television. . . .

Certain books have helped to popularize Plains culture. Black Elk Speaks *is taught most often at the university.* . . .

And even then it's a perversion of what it means to be an Indian in this country—how do you translate context? Within my tribe you have people who are very grounded in the traditions, and are very close to the land. Then you have people who are heavily involved in church; some are involved in both; some live in Tulsa, which is where I grew up; others live all over but are still close to that place which is home. It is more than land—but of the land—a tradition of mythologies, of ongoing history . . . it forms us.

What is there specifically in the Muskogee culture that lends itself to poetry?

That's like asking what is it in life that lends itself to poetry . . . it's the collective myth balanced with history.

When you talk about particulars of individuals and tribes, you are continually breaking down conventions and stereotypes. Does that become tiresome for you?

Yes, it does. I find that wherever I speak I always get asked more questions having to do with culture than with writing.

You must feel like a cultural missionary sometimes. . . .

Right. I feel like I'm having to explain something that's not really easily explainable.

Among your friends, and among the other writers you mentioned, surely you don't have to keep explaining.

No. There's no need. Culture just is. Certainly I'm always asking myself questions about how we came to be, and how we're becoming, and who we are in this world. . . .

In terms of your own background, were there people in your family who loved words? Where does your love of language come from?

Probably from both sides. I have a grandfather, my father's grandfather, who is a full-blooded Creek Baptist minister. I often feel him and I know much of what I am comes from him (including my stubbornness!) I know that he had a love for words and he spoke both Muskogee and English. My mother used to compose songs on an old typewriter. I think she loved the music more than the words, she wasn't particularly a wordsmith, but could translate heartache. From her I learned Patsy Cline, and other "heartbreak country."

Do you remember what made you write that first poetry in your twenties?

Yes, very distinctly. The urge was the same urge I had to make music. Around that time was the first time I heard music in poetry, heard native writers like Leslie Silko, and Simon Ortiz read their work. I also heard Galway Kinnell for the first time, his was one of the first poetry readings I ever attended. I became friends with Leo Romero whose dedication to poetry impressed me. He was always writing and reading his work to me. I witnessed process and began writing my own pieces. Of course, the first attempts were rather weak. Like newborn colts trying to stand just after birth. . . .

You attended the M.F.A. Program in Creative Writing at the University of Iowa. Was that helpful to you?

Well, I have to take into consideration my age when I went—I was in my mid-twenties. I was a single mother. I arrived at this strange country with two small children—my son was seven and my daughter was three. I knew no one, did not know the place, or the people. About the university setting—I felt like I had walked into a strange land in which I had to learn another language. This comes from being of native background, from the West, but it also comes from being a woman in that institution. I heard the director say once to a group of possible funders—I was one of the people they chose to perform for them at a reception—he told them that the place was actually geared for teaching male writers, which is honest; it was true, but I was shocked. I remember Jayne Anne Phillips and I looking at each other, like "can you believe this? Then why are we sitting here?" Certainly I think I learned a lot about technique. I also learned that what was most important in a poem had nothing to do in some ways with what I thought was most important. I felt like the art of poetry had broken down into sterile exercises. And yet, I know I admire some of the work of those people who taught me. But the system had separated itself from the community, from myth, from humanhood.

But you saw it through?

I did see it through. I wanted to walk away. One way I made it through was through the help of people like Sandra Cisneros—through close ties to the Indian and Chicano communities, to the African American community, to women's groups. Sandra and I were also part of a Third World Writers Workshop that also included African American writer Kambon Obayani; Ricardo Longoria, a Smith, Texas, Chicano non-fiction writer; and Pam Durban, a white woman writer from the South.

Have you been able to bring back some of the technical skill you learned to what you consider fundamental?

Yes. You can have the commitment to writing, the fire, but you can write crummy poems. Certainly you need technique. I guess what I'm saying is that I felt values were out of balance.

What was missing?

Heart. And yet some of the poets who taught me there had heart in their poems. But sometimes I felt like what was more important was the facade of being a poet. It became more of an academic pursuit than a pursuit of what it means to live. Granted I was young and I had a lot of misconceptions to work through.

Could you say more about your true teachers of poetry, those who have influenced your work?

I feel like Galway Kinnell has been a teacher, even though I have never met him. I love his work. I think that what he has is a beautiful balance between technique and music. He is such a poet. He's a poet's poet with the music . . . and that's important to me. Of course James Wright. Richard Hugo. Adrienne Rich. I admire her sheer audacity. In the face of everything she learned from the fathers, given the time when she grew up and her own father's admonitions, still she became herself.

I see that in your work, too. I don't know if you are aware of how daring your work is, and how dangerous!

I'd better be! I love the work of Audre Lorde; she has also been one of my teachers.

In the dedication to In Mad Love and War *you affirm that "the erotic belongs in the poetry, as in the self." Can you elaborate?*

It has taken me years to divest myself of Christian guilt, the Puritan cloud that provides the base for culture in this country . . . or at least to recognize the twists and turns of that illogic in my own sensibility. In that framework the body is seen as an evil thing and is separate from spirit. The body and spirit are not separate. Nor is that construct any different in the place from which I write poetry. There is no separation. See Audre Lorde's "Uses of the Erotic: The Erotic as Power" (*Sister Outsider,* Crossing Press, 1984) for a viable definition of the erotic. Again, there is no separation.

Feminist writings and lesbian feminist writings have been very important to you, your work?

Yes, they have.

Are there other writers who have been important to you that we should know about?

Yes. I can think of a lot of writers who are important to me— Leslie Silko, for instance, whom I met shortly after I started writing. I actually took a fiction class from her at UNM as an undergraduate. . . . I especially liked our wine breaks in our office, the stories as we listened to Fleetwood Mac, watched for rain. . . . There are a lot of people . . . Beth Brant, Louis Oliver, June Jordan. . . .

You dedicated the poem "Hieroglyphics" (from In Mad Love and War) *to June Jordan. Why did she get that one?*

Well, it's a long story.

It's a wonderful poem. It moves across time and space, defying boundaries. Maybe June Jordan has a mythic imagination that can comprehend those leaps?

Yeah. I mean she is somebody you can talk to like that and you can't talk to everyone that way. Sometimes in a poem you assume you can.

Maybe you assume that because you need to make the poems accessible. You want people to feel like you are talking to them. In Mad Love and War *is a breakthrough in terms of form and content. How do you feel about being formally inventive?*

I don't know. I don't really know what I'm doing.

You lean into the unknown in those lines and see what happens?

Yes, I do. I don't analyze. I mean certainly analysis is also part of the process of writing poetry, but it's not primary. It comes later in the process.

In part it's probably discipline that lets you explore. Discipline from the habit of years of writing. Do you write daily?

I don't. I try to! [laughter] Well, do you?

No, of course not! We were talking before about having families and having lives, and here you are in Knoxville. I mean, how are you supposed to write every day? Though William Stafford writes every day, even when he's traveling.

Writing is a craft and there's something to doing it or you lose it. I used to paint and draw, and was quite a good artist, but I can't do it at the same level anymore. It's not that I've lost it but I'd have to get my chops together, so to speak, practice.

Do you regret the decision to give up painting?

I don't know that I regret it, but I certainly miss painting. That particular language was more familiar to me than the literary world. . . .

What can you do in poetry that painting could not achieve?

Speak directly in a language that was meant to destroy us.

You have focused on your writing and on your music.

Yes. If I'm not writing I'm thinking about it, or looking at things—I feel this infuses my vision. I'm listening for stories and listening to how words are put together and so on.

Living a "writer's life"?

Yes.

The theme of music gets into your poetry when you dedicate your poems to Billie Holiday or make reference to Coltrane. But I also sense the influence of jazz on your forms.

Well, that wasn't conscious. I think it's coming out of playing the saxophone. I realized recently that I took it up exactly when I entered academe. I don't feel like I've become an academic but if you're going to be in that place, certainly it's going to rub off on you. [laughter]

So you needed some way back to the body?

Yes. Anyway, it was a time when I started teaching at the University of Colorado, Boulder. I had run from teaching in universities. I remember applying once years ago for the University of Texas, El Paso, and then I couldn't make it to MLA for the interview because I had no money. I preferred to keep my own hours, worked freelance, doing screenplay writing and readings and workshops—somehow the money always came in—but it's a tough existence, you have to have a lot of faith. I got a position as assistant professor at the University of Colorado, Boulder. I wrote "We Must Call a Meeting" right after I started teaching there because I was afraid that in that atmosphere, in that place, I was going to lose my poetry. That was around the time I started playing tenor sax. I play tenor and soprano now, but I realize that in a way it was a way to keep that poetry and keep that place.

Keep your sanity, keep your juice!

Yeah. I mean you pick up the saxophone again, I suppose it's like writing poetry, you are picking up the history of that. Playing saxophone is like honoring a succession of myths. . . . I never thought of this before but: the myth of saxophone and here comes Billie Holiday and there's Coltrane. I love his work dearly, especially "A Love Supreme." That song has fed me. And all of that becomes. When you play you're a part of that, you have to recognize those people.

There's a very strong sense of community in your work, community of musicians you address; community of other writers, community of women. . . . I want to ask you about your great-aunt, to whom you dedicated She Had Some Horses.

She's the relative I was closest to, and my life in some ways has uncannily paralleled hers. I miss her dearly. I always felt like I dropped into an alien family almost—maybe most people do—but when she and I got together, then I felt akin. She was very interested in art—she was a painter and was very support-ive of the Creek Nation Council House Museum in Okmul-gee, and donated most of her paintings to them. She traveled. We followed the same routes. Like her, I left Oklahoma for New Mexico—I was sent to an Indian boarding school in Santa Fe. It was a school for the arts, very innovative in its time, sort of like an Indian *Fame* school. When I left Okla-homa to go to high school there, in a way it saved my life. . . .

In my travels I often met relatives of people she knew. I have a necklace that Maria Martinez gave her—Maria, the potter from San Ildefonso. (My great-aunt) was someone who was married for six months and didn't like it and got a divorce, and spent a lot of time driving—she liked traveling Indian country—and also opened a jewelry shop.

So there's movement, dynamism, in your family, and that restlessness. . . .

Yes. Through her and her life I understand myself more clearly, and I love her dearly and miss her.

Did she live long enough to see the book dedicated to her?

No. She died before my father . . . in 1982.

But she knew you were a poet?

Oh yes. She was real proud of that.

What's new in your work that you feel comfortable talking about?

The music, what I've been actively involved in to the tune of two or three hours a night (that's a lot of time!) is working with my band *Poetic Justice*. We're working on a show, putting together performances of my poems.

Earlier you mentioned that you were frustrated about your music—why?

I want to be farther along than I am. The music is still not as far along as the poetry. I fooled around with the sax for about seven years; I've played really seriously for only two years. . . . I want to play more and spend more time with it.

What has the audience response been like?

Our first gig we played in Santa Rosa, California, as part of a show of Indian performers called Indian Airobics, and most recently in Minneapolis. There we were brought in by The Loft. The audiences loved us. We're still rather raw in actual practice, we've very recently come together, but there's something we make as a band with the music and poetry that is rather exciting.

I recently read a selection of autobiographical prose that you did, called "Family Album" (The Progressive, March 1992). Are you still working on the autobiographical writing?

I'm working on a manuscript of autobiographical writings. I call it: "A Love Supreme: Stories, Poems, and Parables." There's much interest in it.

So it's a mixture of several genres. The "Family Album" piece has passages of poetry in it.

Yes, I think it's all one. I work within that assumption.

You mentioned once before that you were putting together a book called "Reinventing the Enemy's Language." Are you still working on that?

Yes. It's an anthology of native women's writings. The original concept was to include writings from North and South America. We have one piece from a native woman from El Salvador. We also received some prose from Rigoberta Menchu as well as from Wilma Mankiller, Cherokee Chief. We have work in it from Canada—it's quite wide-ranging, and includes many genres.

What else is going on with your work? How far did you get with your essay on poetry and jazz?

Oh, it's getting there. I have rewriting, rethinking to do. Some of the pieces are meant particularly for music. We're rearranging and performing two tunes of Jim Pepper's. Jim was a friend of mine, a fine jazz saxophone player who integrated jazz and tribal forms with music. He's the same tribe, Muskogee (or Creek) as well as Kaw Indian from Oklahoma. He died recently and I wanted to play a tribute to him. So we decided on "Witchi Tia To," for which he is most famous, and "Lakota Song"—which isn't an original tune but his arrangement is unique of this Lakota woman's love song. I "sing" the women's part on tenor sax. For "Witchi Tia To" I read a poem as a tribute to him, "The Place the Musician Became a Bear on the Streets of a City Meant to Kill Him."

It's an intimate cosmic dance! You're doing so many things—we haven't touched on all of them—you're active in tribal life, you've been traveling to various tribal ceremonies, you teach, give workshops and readings. How do you find time to do it all? How do you make time for your writing?

I was blessed with energy. I also try to integrate each aspect of my life. The poetry I mix with the music. And so on . . . though sometimes I just lose it. Then get back up again. I get excited about the possibilities and permutations of sound, about the color blue, for instance.

I want to ask you whether there is a connection between poetry and politics, and poetry and prayer? Are these intermingled?

Of course.

In the back of In Mad Love and War, *there's a poem based on a native traditional form. . . .*

Which comes out of the Beauty Way Chant. I used to speak Navajo fairly well. I know that it's influenced my writing.

I've been told that it's a very difficult language.

It's a beautiful language. I love the way that you can say things in that language. So that's been a powerful influence.

How did you learn Navajo?

When I was a student at UNM I took Navajo language for a year and a half. I had a wonderful teacher the first year,

Roseanne Willink, a Navajo from western New Mexico. We had a great time in there. I remember making up jokes and then starting dreaming in Navajo. I don't know my own language and wish to learn.

Was your family bilingual?

No, my father's mother had died when he was young. His father married a white woman. He had a lot of difficulties as a child. He was beaten a lot by his dad and sent to a military school in Ponca City, Oklahoma. I think being Creek—which he was proud of—became a very painful thing for him.

No wonder he had such a hard time coping. You spoke earlier about his alcoholism. He had so much to contend with as such a young person.

Yes, he did. But anyway, back to your earlier question—for me there's always a definite link between poetry and prayer. I think that you can say that a poem is always a prayer for whomever you're speaking of. "Eagle Poem" at the end (of *In Mad Love and War*) is most obviously a prayer. You could look at all poems as being a prayer for our continuance. I mean even the act of writing, to be creative, has everything to do with our continuance as peoples.

Weaving Stories for Food

Interview with Donelle R. Ruwe

"Reconciliation," your tribute to Audre Lorde, was very moving.

"Reconciliation" was an unusual poem for me. It was an extended prayer. I wrote it as a prayer. Really, all poetry is a prayer, you have to go to the center place, inside you, to write poetry.

"Reconciliation" opens up by reinscribing God in very unusual ways. What's happening in that section?

I think about what Alice Walker said in *The Color Purple,* about finding God in that color. The color purple is God praising, a heightened interaction in an ordinary field. God illuminates us with incredible beauty yet is present somewhere at the apex of terror. I can see the workings of God in all that is complex in this life. I never liked the image of God as a white man, which is what was given me in church. With my Muskogee people the image that comes about encompasses the incredible force, the life that pulses through the purple flowers, that pulses toward us through the sun. And that's God.

As a child, I really got into church. It was a refuge from my home life, and I liked the singing, the storytelling. But I was lured into the church with candy. That's one of the tactics for getting people to any kind of meeting, food. I came out one late spring afternoon from kindergarten class and

From *Religion & Literature* 26, no. 1 (Spring 1994).

the church people were handing out flyers attached to suckers. I fell for it. I knew there were more sweets where that came from! So I went to their vacation Bible school where they fed us Koolaid and cookies, sort of like Jim Jones. And I was easy!

But I did love the singing and the storytelling. And as I said it was also a refuge from chaos at home. But it was a very tricky refuge because I never fit in. Everyone knew my dad was Indian, and I was half-Indian. (My mother is one-quarter Cherokee, but I'm enrolled in my father's tribe.) His family were more present for me, still are. I also carried the stigma of my parent's divorce, which happened when I was around eight years old. And the church I went to was like most of the churches in the Bible Belt, very fundamentalist and judgmental in outlook. I always had difficulty with that. The church warned us to stay away from Catholics, they worship graven images. Or "We don't dance," yet David danced joyfully in front of the altar. Dance in the Bible was a celebration of life, like the color purple. I used to ask questions all the time regarding these incongruences. The answers were never satisfactory. Church was a very uncomfortable place to be because I didn't fit in, yet I stayed. It was safer in many ways than home at that time.

When you write about God in your poetry, do you try to revise that Bible Belt fundamentalism? Or are you deliberately distancing yourself from it?

I am reconnecting with the true image of the sacred, I believe. There's no sense engaging evangelical Christianity. You can't engage something like that because they don't encourage interaction and thinking for yourself. I have an uncle I love dearly. He's very musical, but refuses to play anything but hymns. I sent him a tape of my band's music and he refused to listen to it because the music is secular. Yet, if he really listened, interacted, he could hear that we are speaking and singing of the same things. His closed-mindedness is a loss. I've always gone in my own direction, since my first awareness. I've preferred being around my own tribal people, and tribal people of this country and others, around anyone who likes to share stories and songs of the sacred, of our various journeys here. They include everyone from spiritual people of Ghana, Oregon, to my friend Father John Staudenmaier, a practicing Jesuit priest. Others are people I've seen in dreams, not here.

The church isn't foreign in my family. I have a grandfather who was a Creek Baptist minister, whose mission was in Florida with the Seminole. He took the family and went down in the winters. He was quite a brilliant man, at one point was a school superintendent in the Creek nation. I feel him around me often.

"Reconciliation" describes a god who creates but is also created in the poem. This God becomes family, a relative. Is that how you view God or a god?

Well I'd rather have a god who is related than a stranger, than a judgmental god who would destroy people from jealousy.

The Old Testament version—

Which is very alive in Oklahoma [laughter]. The way I understand life is that it is dynamic process. God isn't on a far-removed distant throne. There is no separation, and relativity is the law. So God, then, is a relative, and lives at the root of molecular structure in all life, humans, animals, plant life, minerals as well as in the essence of the sun.

Your recent poetry often refers to molecular structure. What does it mean exactly?

I'm very interested in quantum physics, and feel that the Western world scientists are finally getting out of the mode of the machine age. There are other ways to fly to the moon. NASA is outdated in concept. Matter is dynamic, isn't just hard physical. The dynamic force appears at all levels. I believe that love is the gravity. It keeps us together, keeps us going.

How dynamic is matter? For example, can you transform yourself at the molecular level, or is that something that stays the same?

I think you can transform you consciousness, you know, which is your being, you can transform that to that level.

Let me ask about transformations in "The Place the Musician Became a Bear on the Streets of a City" or in other poems in your books. In Judeo-Christian traditions, ideas of transformation are closely tied to ideas of Christ, to the Incarnation: word made flesh, or the spirit becoming human. But I think transformations in your poetry, and poetry by other American Indians, are very different. Could you comment on this?

Tell me how you read these transformations.

Well, I don't sense a dialogue between the spirit and the flesh. You transform flesh into flesh, a human into a bear. In a similar way, Momaday also talks about transforming into his bear self.

You're describing a transformation between spirit and flesh as if they were separate. I think where theologians get into trouble is that they're working out of a hierarchical structure. There's God sitting at the top of the world, in the image of a man, no women around in that trilogy of God the Father, Son, and Holy Ghost. I propose a different structure; it's not original but what I've learned from being around tribal peoples, and in my own wanderings. The shape is a spiral in which all beings resonate. The bear is one version of human and vice versa. The human is not above the bear, nor is Adam naming the bear. Male and female are equal, useful forces—there's no illusion of domination. We move together. Transformation is really about understanding the shape and condition of another with compassion, not about overtaking.

I believe that words serve that power. Momaday speaks of this as do most native writers who are in the culture(s). It's a basic belief in my poetry. In my poem "Transformations" I attempt to turn hatred into love. But there are simultaneous transformations occurring: there was a man dying, who appears to be dying, yet he is also living in a way he never lived in his life on West 2nd Street in Denver. He's also a butterfly of sorts.

What do butterflies signify in poems such as "The Dawn Appears with Butterflies"? Do they reflect life, or death, or transformation?

They are a symbol of transformation, and their transformation is so startling. I identify, have watched my life transform in such a manner. The butterfly and I then are linked. We are all linked. I've learned from them. Noticed how crucial they are to the growth of corn and other plants, as much as the rain, the sun. Sometimes when they turn in the sun you get a glimpse of the other side.

This world is only part of it, we get clues as to the dynamic possibility around us. The world's been described as a stage, and that analogy works well, but loses dimension and translation especially when you consider the spiral and a butterfly. Yet, though we see the worm change into a butterfly, it sometimes turns back to the worm, for the worm has as much possibility for ecstasy.

This transformation discussion about being able to glimpse the other side reminds me of a statement you made in an earlier interview: you mentioned that American literature has a hard time dealing with anything other than the European concept of the soul—I was fascinated by that comment. What do you think the European concept of the soul is, and what is your own concept?

European is a wide-ranging term and what I mean by that is really a contemporary, industrial age–Euro-American sense of space and time in which there's only the present. It's a very adolescent sense of time. There is no future or past when it comes right down to what I need and want right now. That's what's been demonstrated to native peoples on this continent. And that's what I mean by that, which is really dismissing some incredible traditions out of tribal British Isles, out of tribal European cultures so there's a lot more to that.

But I suppose what I meant goes back to my church, the

church that I went to, in that there's a sense of separation that came about in which the body—you're not to dance, you're not to praise God with the body. I understand lovemaking is praising God with your body. I understand dancing, all these physical things, eating, everything can be. And there's the separation. That's what I was getting at—there's this incredible terrible separation, a gulf between the heart and mind, between the heart and soul, between the soul and the body—which isn't there, it all works together. The body isn't evil, the body's beautiful. The body's not terrible.

I'd like to return to the Audre Lorde memorial poem and ask about the way you use myth and story in your poetry. Are you retelling her story in order to make it present, or to become reconciled to loss?

It's not retelling her story. The title, "Reconciliation," was suggested by the planning committee for the Audre Lorde Memorial in New York City. The poem is a prayer. I am talking to God, something that is especially poignant and loaded after the death of someone who is beloved by so many. She was a mover of large groups of people. She had a particular charge that transformed cultures. When we lose someone such as her (although we never really ever lose anything or anyone), we have to shift to accommodate the change. The poem addressed our collective change.

When I read the poem, I understood that a great many things—the civil rights movement, the American Indian movement—were being linked together around the memory of Audre Lorde.

Because they are. The civil rights movement affected all of us.

It's as if she's being elevated to a mythic position.

In a way she is, but then she isn't. We all have mythic proportions. Let me read this piece, that goes right after this piece, "Witness."

> *The Indian wars never ended in this country. We could date them as beginning with contact by Columbus, an Italian hired by the Spanish court to find the land of spice and gold. Of course we fought intertribally and among ourselves, but a religious fervor large enough to nearly destroy a continent was imported across the Atlantic.*
>
> *We were hated for our difference by our enemies.*
>
> *The civil rights movement awakened many of us to the beauty of our difference. We began to understand how oppression had become our eyes, our ears, our tongues—We rose up together and continued to sing, as we always had, but with more pride, a greater love for ourselves.*
>
> *We were energetic with our remembered love and stood with each other. The tragedies of loss and heartbreak appeared even more terrible at this time.*
>
> *During this reawakening I remember being in the thick of plans for the new world; in coffeehouses, in the pine smell of mountain retreats, on the road. We are still working on them.*

We're together, all part of the movement, we're all children of that movement, if we're not actually participants. I think people are born together at a certain time and for certain reasons to work out these differences.

The poem ends by talking about the four directions. Each direction seems to connect to different parts of the civil rights movements: for American Indians, the West with battlegrounds; for African Americans, the North with unfulfilled hope.

I wanted to end with the East, with the sunrise, because it is a point of return, of beginning. I started with the South first, and then went back clockwise to the East.

I'd like to ask you about myth. For me, myths are stories—some are interesting, and some less interesting and you can analyze them or ignore them. Clearly, that is not how myth works for you or in your writing. What does myth mean to you?

I believe myth is an alive, interactive event that is present in the everyday. Certainly stories are a reference, manipulated and changed by the needs of the storyteller as well as the audience. I understand myth to be at the root of all event. It's the shimmering framework for all else to occur. It's dense and light at the same time. Rabbit, the trickster, is present in all of us. And Rabbit would not be if not for us poor humans and our particular frailties as humans.

In "The Place the Musician Became a Bear on the Streets of a City," you seem to be using myth in a certain way, rewriting myth to include contemporary society: "rearranging song to include the subway hiss under your feet." Even so, it seems that you're not only rewriting myth, you're also rewriting Brooklyn.

I don't think humans write and rewrite myth, it's an interactive process. Perhaps humans are being rewritten by myth. The dynamic relationship is everywhere. The rain clouds respond to us, and we respond to them. Many cultures have nurtured this relationship. It's like any other thing that's nourished and taken care of, the relationship flourishes.

In different tribal cultures, women are often the storytellers, the ones who transmit culture and myth. Do see yourself as a storyteller? What are the stories you're trying to voice?

I don't consider myself a storyteller. I do tell stories as part of my poetry but I am not a storyteller in the traditional sense of the word. I call Leslie Silko a storyteller, but she says she's not a storyteller either, not in the tribal sense of the term as one living within the heart of the culture weaving stories for food for the community. Yet, I see Leslie doing that, from the borders of cultures. She weaves them together. So she is a storyteller.

June Jordan spoke at Notre Dame earlier this week, and I asked her, since you often talk about her influence on her work, if she saw any similarities between her writing and your writing. She said that her writing has to always stay with what's out there; she must stick to reality. You, on the other hand, don't tell the truth—you're a visionary. *Could you comment on that?*

Well, I think I tell the truth. We're telling the same truth, but we go at it in very different angles. And I think I've given myself more permission to move differently. I've always felt that my inner landscape is a much larger and more visible present. I mean, who knows why it comes about—and why you go through what you go through, but that was always the landscape in which I moved more easily and more gracefully. And it's really only recently that I've felt like I've been fully present, and realized I could be fully present here without losing my place. So it's very interesting, I have talked a lot, I don't talk a lot in interviews about it—but that world is very intense, and I feel like I move in and out of time and places. I don't know if it's reincarnation, that's a possibility, but it's also possible that all really exists all at once, and that there are ways to move in and out of the different stories, and different ways of experiencing the stories.

A Laughter of Absolute Sanity

Interview with Angels Carabi

You have said that you are an "enrolled member" of the Creek tribe. Can you explain what that means?

That term has become used very recently, and it has to do with the controversy among Indian people regarding who is Indian and who is not. This issue has come out because of history, because of dealings with the U.S. government, state governments, and others. There is certainly a cultural definition of who is an Indian, and this is based on who belongs to the tribe and who the tribal members recognize as such. This classification doesn't always coincide with that of the federal government because tribes have different criteria. With the rise of popularity of Indians in the "new age," there have been a lot of people—they are called "wannabes"—who claim to be Native Americans even though they may only have some faint, unsubstantiated claim to a fraction of blood. Nowadays, there is a proliferation of people in academic communities, even some writers who by blood are only an eighth or a sixteenth Indian, who call themselves "Indian writers," although they don't know their tribe or their family members. They don't really have any connection with their people, except for some name on a piece of paper that goes two or three generations back.

From *Belles Lettres: A Review of Books by Women* 9, no. 4 (Summer 1994).

Your father is a Creek.

Yes, my father is Creek, and my mother is Cherokee, although she is not an enrolled member because her grandmother refused to sign any papers that the white man gave. She was a rebel and was raised by full bloods in Oklahoma. My mother is Cherokee and she is also French and Irish, so her background is very mixed.

You try to reconcile such polarities, and I think you develop this concept quite clearly in your poem "She Had Some Horses."

Yes. The poem says "She had some horses she loved / she had some horses she hated / These were the same horses." Yes, my poetry is a way to bring together the paradoxes in the world. You are a poet when you understand paradox; when you become a human being, you understand paradox. At first, I thought that there was no way to reconcile polarities. For instance, initially, I thought of myself as being either totally white or totally Indian, and that there was no way to bring together these forces. The paradox was in my own blood, in my own body. It was difficult to decide for one or the other because I loved and hated both parts of myself. As a poet, I learned to bring all this despairing history together. For me, poetry is a bridge over the sea of paradox, the sea is the blood, and it becomes a way to join them. It has value and a promise.

In your poetry you express a sense of connectedness of all things.

A common belief to all tribal people is that the world is alive; absolutely everything is connected. It's what Leslie Silko talks about in *Ceremony,* about the world being fragile, about Thought Woman spinning the web of life and creating everyone. Eight years ago, I had a dream in which I saw this web of life. Someone was teaching me, and I was taken to a point outside the speed of the Earth and I saw this web. It was incredible; it was like pulsating life. You could observe how everyone, absolutely everyone, was together in this incredible web, and how what one person said or thought or did affected the web immediately. It was quite an incredible view. There were connections between the people in Spain and the people in Oklahoma. It was a direct connection in which time was not separated by minutes or hours, but by thinking of someone you could be with that person immediately. So, in that way, time mattered not at all. Given that, and what I understand about life, yes, I believe that everything is connected in a timeless fashion.

The moon is a central image in your work. To me it evokes the circle in which everything is contained and every single part is equally important.

The moon represents ceremony, as well as the memory of Earth. We count time by looking at the moon; it represents cycle.

In Indian culture, life and death are seen as a continuum, parts of a cycle.

Yes. I don't think that we appear suddenly in the world from nowhere and suddenly disappear. If I look at the natural world, things don't occur that way. I know that there is a world of spirits. I know that there is a world of going after. I have been there. I cannot prove it scientifically.

In Indian culture, the supernatural world is an essential part. Toni Morrison once told me that, for her, the supernatural world was "another form of knowing." Would you agree with this perception?

Yes. The supernatural world is ingrained in our culture and it is another way of knowing. Something that I like about Morrison's work is that she incorporates that world—which runs parallel to the factual one—but she manages to weave it in and out. What is fantastic about *Beloved* is that what she is doing represents the "real" world. In European culture the world is supposed to have only three dimensions. It's constructed in a way that only the five senses can maneuver.

There are probably more than five senses; there are probably ten, twelve, fourteen, a hundred senses—and we haven't developed them.

The mythical world is very alive and very rich. I feel that I learn from that world as much as from this one. Visions and dreams have told me more about what it means to be alive, what it means to be here, on this planet, than any book I have read, yet books can also point the way.

I remember my dreams since childhood, and I have been in many places in them. One dream that is very important, now that I have been to Spain, is one in which a man from Spain came to visit me. He told me that he had been waiting to see me for a long time. And I realized then that he was part of myself. He showed me the history of the conquistadores and the Indian people. Over the images of blood and destruction was an incredible light, which was the huge power of the sun coming through. It was illuminating a terrible reality yet it was setting it to rest; and the underlying concept was forgiveness. I don't quite know how to express it—maybe one of these days I'll paint it or do it in music—but it was like a whole painting, almost like a hologram of images that he showed me. It was centuries deep, and yet it was all contained in one time and space, and I was part of it.

The ceremony of the Green Corn dance is about forgiveness. Does it have anything to do with the underlying theme in your dream?

I'm sure it does. The Green Corn becomes a very powerful symbol, an image that resonates in the present. Every time that it takes place, it carries the power of all the ancestors.

It's a cleansing ceremony.

Yes, it is. Forgiveness is part of renewal. It represents the renewal of people, and at that time you are to forgive those who need to be forgiven.

Do you incorporate the mythical world into your everyday life?

I think myths incorporate me into their everyday life. I think that a reciprocal process happens, maybe because I am a poet or a woman. I always wear the mythical world around or inside and feel things directly out of it.

Do you see your poetry as having a healing power in the tradition of Indian chanting?

I think some of it does. One of the poems in *In Mad Love and War* is a poem to heal a sore throat; another is a transformation that tries to bring people into love, and another is to do away with fear. "Eagle Poem" is a prayer. I don't think poems are static. I see them as alive forms of dynamic energy.

You play the saxophone. Does music play a role in your poetic perception of life?

I guess it always has. I was always doing music, even as a poet; often the poems would come out to me first by sound. Certainly images are very important, and sometimes I think I write like a painter. But sound is always important; sound that is like music would come to me, with rhythm. Someone said to me—even before I played the saxophone—that I performed my poetry as if I were playing saxophone because of the pauses. I don't think that music and poetry are that separated. The origin of poetry is really songs.

It is my understanding that Indian music was primarily functional, that is to say, used for some purpose—for instance, to call the rain. Does it continue to be like that?

Yes. What you make is for some kind of use. This could be eating soup or bringing rain, and both are important. I see my work in the same tradition. I wrote a poem to help my daughter when she turned thirteen. It's very much a part of that. As a poet, I don't want to separate myself from the world, but to include myself.

Silko, in Ceremony, *says that one of the worst evils that can happen to a people is to forget—to forget one's own traditions, one's own culture. Would you agree with this?*

Yes. I agree, because it is what we are made of, the stories that we carry with us. Stories create us. We create ourselves with stories. Stories that our parents tell us, that our grandparents tell us, or that our great-grandparents told us, stories that reverberate through the web.

Did you grow up listening to stories told by your relatives?

A lot of my relatives died very young. I don't have people in my family that lived up to their eighties or nineties. My father died when he was in his fifties, so I am aware of this leak. However, I was taught in my dreams, and my aunt told me lots of stories.

What is your view on maintaining Indian traditions? Silko indicates that traditional ceremonies must adapt to modern times to have value.

I think that any culture is a living thing, and it adapts and grows. Anything that remains static dies. It's the same for Indian cultures. What is important is to have a voice in those changes and adapt them so they become regenerative to the culture rather than destructive. It's like pruning a tree or a bush. If you prune it too much you kill it, but if you do it right it grows twice as full. It becomes a ceremony.

Can you talk about the role of memory? In Native American litera-ture, memory is usually presented as a nurturing force.

Memory for me becomes a big word. It's like saying "world." Memory is the nucleus of every cell; it's what runs, it's the gravity, the gravity of the Earth. In a way, it's like the stories themselves, the origin of the stories, and the continuance of all the stories. It's this great pool, this mythic pool of knowledge and history that we live inside.

Do you think that the younger generations, for instance, your granddaughter, will be able to continue this tradition of storytelling and preserve the value of memory?

I think so. It's part of her, and it is up to me to convey how important it is to her, to them. That's been the role of grandmothers.

In your poems you talk about a sense of loss, of displacement. How do Indian cultures deal with this sense of loss?

I think that what I do in my work is to interweave elements of the past, the present, and the future. I claim the past, and Silko does it too, and Morrison. I am not talking about data. Morrison, for instance, gave more sense of the history of Afro-American people with her novel *Beloved* than any history book could do, because her book is very human, and very terrible. It's terrifying to enter what I call the psychic wound of the Americas, because it's filled up with that loss. But you have to claim the past. It's filled with stories that move you and, at the same time, horrify you. A friend of mine told me a story about a young Navajo boy, about four years old, who was in his home; his mother wasn't there, and some relatives were supposed to be babysitting. But they began drinking and left the house. The boy got scared, then took his eighteen-month-old baby sister and went walking to his grandmother's. On his way there, she felt too heavy so he left the baby on the road. When he arrived at his grandmother's, he collapsed and went to sleep. The baby was found in blood; apparently, she had tried to crawl back to her house. That's our history. That's history right there. Everything you need to know about colonization and what happened is right there. And I want my writing to reflect that, to make my life congruous with my writing. When you are able to articulate something that is terrible that is inside you, that lives in you, and you no longer deny it, you are able to bring regeneration. Unless you do that, the whole planet is going to be destroyed, I think.

So something that could be extremely painful actually brings life.

Yes.

Indian writers—Louise Erdrich, Leslie Silko, and yourself—talk about the consequences of that loss in the present, such as alcoholism and violence. Will the Native American people be able to overcome this situation?

Alcoholism is an epidemic in native people, and I write about it. I was criticized for bringing it up, because some people want to present a certain image of themselves. But again, it comes back to what I was saying: part of the process of healing is to address what is evil. Evil causes disease, when something isn't settled. The very process of the healing is talking about it and recognizing it. Alcoholism is hiding, it comes out of an inability to speak. It's like Tayo in *Ceremony;* not until he has been with Betonie is he able to talk. One has to find the place for his own voice, and Tayo finds that place in Betonie's ceremony.

Let's talk about racism. It seems to me that what lies at the very essence of racism is fear—fear of losing power, fear that your culture is under threat—and that fear makes you ultimately destroy "the other." Would you agree with this?

Yes, I think that—as you say—fear is the cause of racism. Fear of oneself. You don't try to control another group by any deviant means—and racism is a deviant means—unless you are afraid of yourself, unless you feel insecure about your own power. When I talk to groups of young Indians, I tell them that it is important to remember that it's not them who are of less worth, but that it is the person with the racism. So, I tell them that the next time they are in a restaurant, or in a store, and they are treated as a lesser people, they must turn it back in their mind—just give it back. I don't mean act racist, but in their mind say: "This is your weakness, this is not mine." And this is the hardest [thing] to remember, because what happens is that you take it in, and it makes you feel shameful.

I'm light skinned and I have not been subjected as much to racism as my sisters or other relatives of mine have but I have, for instance, not been served in restaurants. It is absurd to treat anyone else as less than a human being because you belong to a different culture, a different race.

Maybe it's impossible for people to transcend the differences, but I don't think so. I think there is common human ground. There was a time in my tribe when people were treated according to how they were as human beings. That was what your value was based on, not if you were dark or had lighter skin or medium skin. It was how you treated other human beings, how you treated the relatives. Nowadays there is something wrong in the world; to be a leader of the people is not based on how much she or he loves the people but on how much power or money one has. It is an insane world. And this is what Silko deals with in *Almanac of the Dead*. The way the Western world is going is terrifying.

Your poetry is metaphysical, but it is also very much concerned with social issues; it's political. You feel that you have a social responsibility towards what is happening in the world.

I don't think that a poet can separate herself or himself from the world that she or he lives in. The poet is charged with the role of being the truth teller of the culture, of the times. I think that this is true for any poet in any culture. I have done other kinds of writing—stories, for instance—but there is something about poetry that demands the truth, and you cannot separate the poem from your political reality. It's all part of the same continuum.

Laughter is also present in your works. "We are in the belly of a laughing god," you say in one poem.

I think that Indian people have one of the most developed senses of humors I've ever heard. You get a lot of this in the writing. It's interesting; the writing tends to be much more heavy and intense, and the laughter becomes a release. You get Indian people together, and it is constant laughter, teasing, and joking—very self-deprecating humor, and that's central to the culture.

In the middle of all the tension and destruction, there is a laughter of absolute sanity that might sound like someone insane. Maybe laughter is the voice of sense. I always tell my students that you cannot take everything too seriously because it will kill you. If you carry bitterness and hatred around, it gives you arthritis, rheumatism, cancer. Certainly, I have to be aware of everything that is happening, but I can't let it kill me.

UNDER DISCUSSION
Donald Hall, General Editor

Volumes in the Under Discussion series collect reviews and essays about individual poets. The series is concerned with contemporary American and English poets about whom the consensus has not yet been formed and the final vote has not been taken. Titles in the series include:

A forthcoming volume will examine the work of Gwendolyn Brooks.
Please write for further information on available editions and current prices.

Ann Arbor

The University of Michigan Press